IRAN

A SHORT HISTORY

The town of Qum

D1517524

From Islamization
to the Present

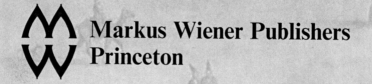
Markus Wiener Publishers
Princeton

IRAN
A SHORT HISTORY

Monika Gronke

Translated from German by Steven Rendall

Second printing, 2009.

The translation of this work was supported by a grant from the
Goethe-Institut, which is funded by the Ministry of Foreign Affairs.

The first German edition of this book was published in 2003;
the second, revised, and updated edition was published in 2006.

For information, write to Markus Wiener Publishers
231 Nassau Street, Princeton, NJ 08542
www.markuswiener.com

Library of Congress Cataloging-in-Publication Data

Gronke, Monika.
  [Geschichte Irans. English]
  Iran : a short history / Monika Gronke ; translated from German
by Steven Rendall.
  Includes bibliographical references and index.
  ISBN 978-1-55876-444-6 (hardcover : alk. paper)
  ISBN 978-1-55876-445-3 (paperback : alk. paper)
  1. Iran—History—640- I. Title.
  DS272.G7613 2007
  955—dc22   2007033337

Markus Wiener Publishers books are printed in
the United States of America on acid-free paper,
and meet the guidelines for permanence and durability
of the Committee on Production Guidelines for
Book Longevity of the Council on Library Resources.

Contents

Introduction

In 628, the sources would have us believe, a letter from the Prophet Muhammad arrived in Ctesiphon, the ancient Sasanian capital on the Tigris. This letter urged the Great King of Persia to convert to Islam, and it inaugurated a new era, although contemporaries were surely not aware that this was so. Only a few years later the Arabs, inspired by their new religion, overthrew the Sasanian Empire, which then became part of the Islamic world. The Arab conquest was the most profound rupture in the history of Iran, and may even be a unique historical phenomenon. It led to a whole people abandoning its own manifold religious tradition and adopting a new faith. Iran became an Islamic country, and it made this momentous change in a relatively short time, in comparison with its long past. However, during the intervening period of more than a thousand years, the Islamic history of Iran has shown that the country was not absorbed by the massive Islamic expansion of the seventh century, nor did it completely forget its pre-Islamic history. Instead, it blended Islam, which was originally alien to it, with its own ancient heritage to create a unique Iranian-Islamic culture. Over the centuries, the latter set its stamp on large parts of the Islamic world, and also inspired a number of works by European writers, among which Goethe's *West-Östlicher Divan* is one of the best known and finest.

The territory of present-day Iran (officially the Islamic Republic) includes an area about one-sixth that of the United States, and its latitude is roughly that of the southern United States. It is a land of high mountains and dry, desert-like basins between the Caspian Sea—which is actually an enormous inland lake with no outlet to the ocean—in the north and the Persian Gulf in the south. The Iranian high plateau is surrounded in the north by the lofty Alburz Mountains, in the west by the Zagros Mountains, which broaden into parallel ranges stretching toward the southeast, and in the east by a mountain range running along the border with Afghanistan and Pakistan and merging in the north with the Hindu Kush. Smaller mountain ranges divide this central highland into several large basins of differing sizes. These basins most commonly consist of gravel and salt deserts like the Kavir Desert and the Lut Desert to the south, with completely sterile salt plains. The few rivers mostly peter out in the gravelly debris of these low places. Iran is primarily a dry land of low rainfall where since antiquity agriculture has been dependent on artificial irrigation. Farming without irrigation was and is possible only in a few areas such as the lowlands near the Caspian.

During long periods of its history in Islamic times, the sphere of Iranian culture nonetheless extended far beyond the geographical borders of the present-day Iran. Mesopotamia—which had been part of the Sasanian Empire, while the emperor's residence was in Ctesiphon, not far from the later site of Baghdad, the capital of the ʿAbbasid caliphate (749-1258)—also belonged to the Iranian cultural sphere, as did the region corresponding to present-day Afghanistan and Transoxania, that is, the land between the Amu Darya and Syr Darya rivers (in ancient times, these were known as the Oxus and the Jaxartes). The name "Iran" is derived from Middle Persian, *Iran*, whose complete form was *Iranshahr* or *Iranzamin* ("Land of the Aryans"; *Iran* is the genitive plural of *ir*, "Aryan"). Although the concept "Aryan" was already found in the ancient Persian Empire of the Achaemenids (558-330 BC), *Iran* first became an established, meaningful term referring to a political, religious, and ethnic unit under the Sasanian dynasty (224-651), the last pre-Islamic dynasty on Persian soil. After the Arab conquest, the country of Iran—which was now part of the extensive Islamic empire—no longer represented a clearly defined territory, but instead disintegrated into individual provinces with their own names (such as Khurasan, Fars, and Azerbaijan), whereas the old term *rân* survived as a historical name for the Sasanian Empire. Persia appears in Firdawsi's so-called Iranian "national epic," the *Shahnameh* ("Book of Kings," c. AD 1000) under the old name *Iranzamin*, which was directly derived from the Middle Persian original. However, "Iran" first reappears as the name of an empire under the rule of the Mongols in the thirteenth century. Since then, the concept "Iran" has been connected with the idea of the greatness and unity of Persia, an idea into which later dynasties, and finally that of the Pahlavis (1925-1979), tried to breathe life. The term "Persia," on the other hand, referred originally to an area in the southwest part of the country, the Old Persian Parsa, which the Greeks called "Persis" and the Arabs "Fars"; it was therefore a purely geographical concept.

Iran's lengthy pre-Islamic past, during which there were three great Persian empires—the Achaemenid, the Parthian, and the Sasanian—may be responsible for the fact that today historians often tend to see Iran as a unity in Islamic times as well, and to seek everywhere for signs of an Iranian national feeling distinguishing Iranians from other peoples. On this view, Arabs and Iranians are fundamentally inimical groups; after their initial conquest by the Arabs, the Iranians are supposed to have later achieved a new national assertiveness under native Persian dynasties. This kind of thorough-going nationalist interpretation of Iranian history inevitably leads to a distorted picture, since it applies a narrowly defined concept in modern European history to ancient periods that were shaped by entirely different factors. Similarly, it overlooks the fact that even in antiquity Iran was a multi-ethnic state and remains one today, and thus cannot be seen as a nation connected with a single people. However, in the course of Persia's pre-Islamic history, political and cultural traditions as well as a peculiarly Iranian idea of the state and ruling power emerged, and these unified the Iranian cultural sphere and lent it its special characteristics. At least as ideas, these traditions survived the Islamization of Persia, and they contributed to the development of a peculiarly Iranian variant of Islamic culture. The consciousness of a great past expressed itself in Iranians' marked sense of superiority both with regard to other peoples, even if the latter subjected Iran to their rule—as did Arabs, Turks, and Mongols—and in Iranian-Islamic literature. The Iranians' adherence to their own traditions is shown with particular clarity by the fact that although like other peoples they ultimately abandoned their ancient religion, they did not give up their language. Persian is the only language in the areas of the Middle East conquered by the Arabs that not only survived this upheaval but early on established its position alongside Arabic as a major language in the Islamic cultural sphere.

This book will describe the chief processes of development and change that have shaped Iran's history since its Islamization, and that have given the country its present character. The material is divided into four main chapters, each defined temporally and dealing with an extensive historical period during which important changes and shifts in direction can be observed.

The first of these periods stretches from the Arab conquest of Iran, which culminated in the Muslim victory at the Battle of Nihavand (642), to the Saljuqs' conquest of Baghdad, the capital of the caliphate (1055). During this period, the ʿAbbasid caliphate came to power and did much to establish the contours of "classical" medieval Islamic culture. This culture was greatly indebted to pre-Islamic Iranian culture. The period was, however, characterized by frequent conflicts over the question of legitimate rule.

With the Saljuqs began the centuries-long influx from Inner Asia into Iran of Turkish and later Mongol nomads; in 1258 the latter overthrew the ʿAbbasid caliphate. This period was characterized by increasing nomadism and economic decline in many parts of the country, but also by brilliant achievements in art and literature.

In 1501, the Safavids put an end to Iran's political fragmentation by reunifying it and making Shiʿism the state religion. The conversion to Shiʿism divided Iran from its Sunni neighbors, but in the long run it also lent the country's various peoples a new spiritual unity. For Iran, the modern age began with the Safavids: diplomatic contacts with Europe were established, economic and commercial relationships broadened.

After further political division in the eighteenth century, military and economic confrontation with the European powers began around the turn of the nineteenth century under the Qajar dynasty. This fourth period is marked by debate regarding the idea of a national state, the secularization of public life, and increasing interest in pre-Islamic Iran. Since the Islamic Revolution ended the country's long monarchical tradition in 1979, Iran has been seeking a new way for itself, for the time being under the rule of Shiʿite religious scholars.

Because of the length of Iranian-Islamic history and the multiplicity of historical materials, a Western historian who wishes to provide a wide readership with a brief history of Iran from Islamization to the present inevitably encounters the difficult question of what can be omitted without doing excessive damage to the overall picture. I have nevertheless decided to attempt such an overview because I hope to contribute to a better understanding of the historical development of one of the most important countries in the Islamic East. If this book makes the long history of Iran and the fascinating culture it has produced since its Islamization more familiar to its readers, leading them to further investigation, it will have achieved its purpose.

Chronology

632	Death of the Prophet Muhammad in Medina.
632–661	Age of the four "righteous caliphs": Abu Bakr (reigned 632-634), ʿUmar (reigned 634-644), Uthman (reigned 644-656), ʿAli (reigned 656-661).
642	Muslim victory in the Battle of Nihavand leads to the conquest of Iran.
651	Assassination of the last Sasanian king, Yazdgard III.
661–749	Umayyad caliphate with its center in Damascus.
680	Battle of Karbala; death (martyrdom) of the third imam, Husayn.
749–1258	ʿAbbasid caliphate with its center in Baghdad, founded 762.
821–873	Tahirids in Khurasan, the first autonomous Islamic dynasty on Iranian soil. 867–903 Safarids in Sistan; 867-901, rule over almost all Iran.
892–999	Samanids in Transoxania and Khurasan; center in Bukhara.
945–1055	Buyids in Iraq and Iran; 945, conquest of Baghdad; greatest extent of the empire under Adud al-Dawla (reigned 978-983).
977–1186	Ghaznavids in Khurasan, Afghanistan, and North India; greatest extent of the empire under Mahmud of Ghazna (ruled 998-1030).
1040–1195	Saljuqs; 1055, conquest of Baghdad; greatest extent of the empire under Malik-Shah (reigned 1073-1092) in Iraq and Iran.
1071	Saljuq victory over Byzantium at the Battle of Manzikert opens up Anatolia for Islam.

1090–1256   Isma'ili sect of the Assassins takes control of
             Alamut Fortress in the Alburz Mountains; Hasan-i
             Sabbah (d. 1124) leader of the Isma'ilis.

1092   Assassination of the Saljuq vizier Nizam al-Mulk.

1200–1220   Khwarazm shahs; 1200-1220, rule over all Iran and
             Transoxania.

1219–1224   Mongols under Genghis Khan (d. 1227) devastate
             Transoxania and Iran.

1256–1335   Rule of the Mongol Il-Khans in Iran.

1258   Overthrow of the Baghdad caliphate by the
             Il-Khan Hülegü.

1295   The Il-Khan Ghazan (reigned 1295-1304) converts
             to Islam; Islam becomes once again the principle
             of rulership.

1370–1405   Timur's campaign of conquest in Transoxania
             and Iran.

1380–1469   Kara Koyunlu (Turkmen tribal confederation) in
             northern and central Iran; greatest extent of the
             empire under Jihan Shah (reigned 1438-1467).

1396–1508   Ak Koyunlu (Turkmen tribal confederation) in
             eastern Anatolia and Iran; greatest extent of the
             empire under Uzun Hasan (reigned 1501-1534).

1405–1506   Rule of the Timurids in Transoxania and Iran.

1501   Isma'il I (reigned 1501–1524) conquers Tabriz
             and proclaims Twelver Shi'ism as the state religion
             of Iran.

1501–1722   Safavids in Iran; centers in Tabriz, Qazvin,
             and Isfahan.

1514   Safavids defeated by Ottoman artillery at the Battle
             of Chaldiran.

1639   By the Treaty of Zuhab (Qasr-i Shirin), Iran loses
             Iraq and the Shi'ite shrines to the Ottoman
             Empire.

1722	The Afghan Ghalzais attack Iran; abdication of the last Safavid shah, Sultan Husayn (reigned 1694-1722).
1722–1736	Nadir Khan drives back the Afghans; nominal rule of two Safavid princes.
1736–1796	Nadir Shah (reigned 1736-1747) and his descendants (Afsharids) in Iran; after 1750, only in northern and central Iran.
1750–1794	Southern Iran under the Iranian Zand dynasty; center in Shiraz.
1779–1925	Qajars in Iran; center in Tehran.
1801–1813	First war between Russia and Iran; 1813, Treaty of Golestan, by which Iran loses large areas of the Caucasus to Russia.
1826–1828	Second war between Russia and Iran; the Treaty of Turkmanchay (1828) and further territorial losses in the Caucasus establish the present border with Russia.
1857	By the Treaty of Paris Nasir al-Din Shah Qajar agrees to recognize the independence of Afghanistan.
1872	Partition of the province of Sistan between Iran and Afghanistan.
1879	Establishment of the Persian Cossack Brigade.
1891–1892	Tobacco boycott.
1906	Victory of the Constitutional Revolution; first parliamentary elections and signing of the constitution for a constitutional monarchy.
1907	Signing of amendments to the constitution.
1911	End of the Constitutional Revolution; the constitution is suspended.
1925–1979	Pahlavi dynasty: Reza Shah (reigned 1925-1941), Muhammad Reza Shah (reigned 1941-1979).

1951–1953   Muhammad Mosaddeq attempts to nationalize the
             Iranian oil industry.

1963   In June, Ayatollah Ruhollah Khomeini (1902-1989)
             calls for resistance to the shah; shah has
             subsequent popular protests put down.

1971   Celebration in Persepolis of 2,500 years of
             Iranian Monarchy.

1979   Islamic Revolution and overthrow of the shah.
             April 1, official proclamation of the Islamic
             Republic of Iran; December 2-3, adoption of the
             constitution by plebiscite.

1980–1988   Iran-Iraq war.

1989   Death of Ayatollah Khomeini. Revision of the
             constitution.

1997   Election of Muhammad Khatami as the fifth
             president of the Islamic Republic.

2005   Election of Mahmud Ahmadinejad as the sixth
             president of the Islamic Republic.

CHAPTER I

The Early Islamic Period (642–1055)

Master/teacher and his student

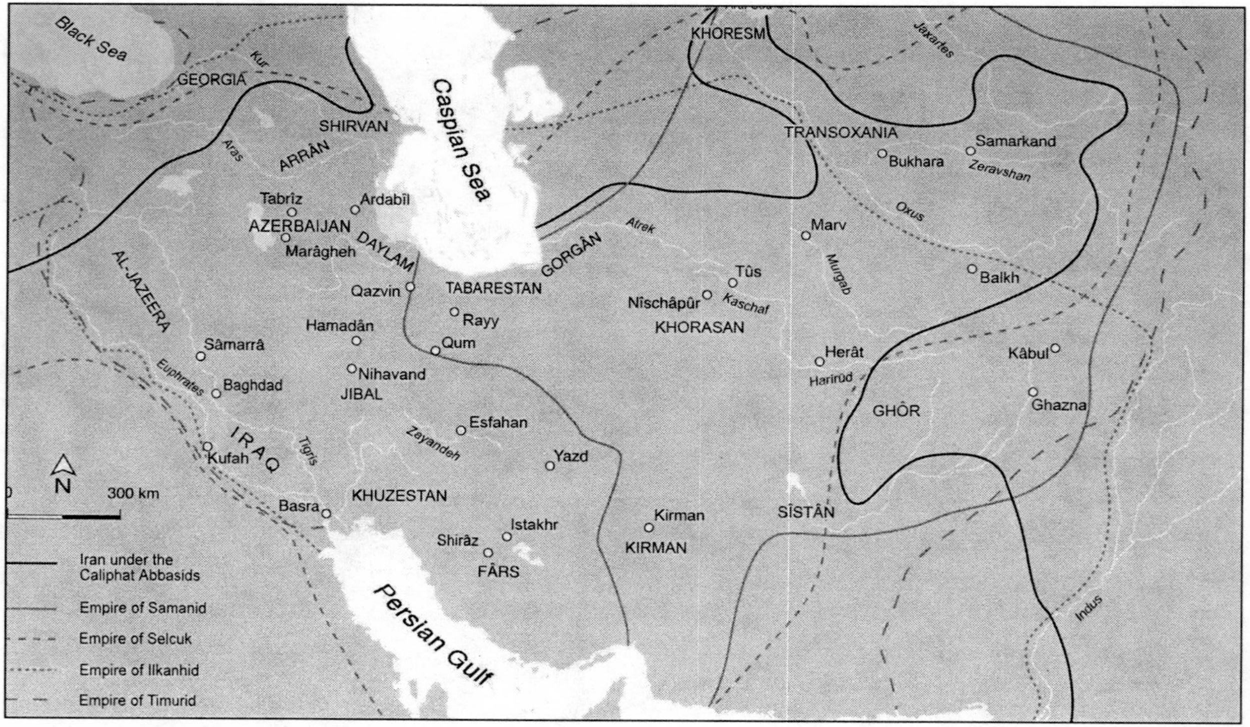
Black Sea
Caspian Sea
Persian Gulf
GEORGIA
Kur
SHIRVAN
Aras
ARRÂN
Tabrîz
Ardabîl
AZERBAIJAN
Marâgheh
DAYLAM
AL-JAZEERA
Qazvin
TABARESTAN
GORGÂN
Atrek
Rayy
Hamadân
Qum
Sâmarrâ
Nihavand
Euphrates
Baghdad
JIBAL
IRAQ
Tigris
Zayandeh
Esfahan
Kufah
Yazd
300 km
N
Basra
KHUZESTAN
Istakhr
Shirâz
FÂRS
Kirman
KIRMAN
KHORESM
TRANSOXANIA
Jaxartes
Samarkand
Bukhara
Zeravshan
Oxus
Marv
Murgab
Tûs
Nîschâpûr
Kaschaf
KHORASAN
Balkh
Herât
Harirûd
Kâbul
Ghazna
GHÔR
SÎSTÂN
Indus
Iran under the Caliphat Abbasids
Empire of Samanid
Empire of Selcuk
Empire of Ilkanhid
Empire of Timurid

Iran from the 7th to the 15th century

The Arab Conquest

Islam is the youngest of the three monotheistic world religions. It was founded by the Prophet Muhammad (c. 570-632) on the Arabian peninsula. Islam proclaims belief in a single God, whom Muhammad named "Allah" (in Arabic, "the God," that is, the one and only God), and maintains that it is the original revelation of God. According to Muhammad, over time God has made his unvarying revelation known to the peoples of the earth through a series of prophets, to the Jews through Moses and to the Christians through Jesus; in Islam's strictly monotheistic conception, Jesus was a prophet, and not the son of God. However, Muhammad, who had come in contact with Jews and Christians living in Arabia, was convinced that in the course of history Judaism and Christianity had deviated from the original divine revelation and that both had retained only an incomplete and distorted version of it. It is Muhammad, seen as the last of the series of prophets, who restores the original divine revelation and thereby concludes it. Islam's sense of superiority to all other religions, including the other monotheistic ones, is based on this claim to have brought men back to the original divine message.

Just two years after the Prophet's death, Muslim Arabs set
out on campaigns of conquest and quickly subjugated
Byzantine Syria and Egypt as well as the whole Persian
Empire of the Sasanians. The defeat of the Sasanian army
in 637 at the battle of al-Qadisiyya on the Euphrates, where
Rustam, the imperial commander-in-chief, was killed, left
the Arabs in control of Iraq and the Sasanian capital, Ctesiphon. In 642, the Arabs won a decisive victory at Nihavand,
in western Iran; in 644 they took Isfahan and in 649 Istakhr,
which had been built on the site of the ancient Persepolis;
starting in 650, they subdued the northern province of
Khurasan. The last Sasanian king, Yazdgard III, fled and
was murdered in 651. Thus the whole territory of the
Sasanian Empire was henceforth under Arab control and
became part of the Islamic realm.

Many reasons have been given for the astonishing speed
of Arab expansion: the Sasanian Empire's internal instability during the crucial period of conquest (the empire had
been exhausted by a long war with Byzantium that had only
recently ended); the unifying and motivating effect of Islam
that inspired the Arabs in their campaigns, especially since
those who fell in battle were promised immediate entrance
into Paradise; the Arabs' mobility and gift for military
improvisation, which gave them an advantage over the slow-
moving Sasanian mercenaries; the nearly unlimited supply
of fighters from the Arabian heartland; and the fact that the
Sasanians seem to have initially underestimated the Arab
advance and considered it just another of the regular but
not really dangerous attacks on the empire. However, a truly
decisive and for the most part overlooked basis for Arab

expansion was the support—despite all the warfare—for Muslims among both Arabs living on the borders of the Sasanian Empire and the native Persian population. This was connected first of all with the status of the so-called *ahl al-kitab* ("People of the Book"). In the Muslim view, human beings were divided into three groups: (1) Muslims, (2) pagans, and (3) Jews and Christians. Jews and Christians could not be put on the same level as the pagans, because they were both in possession of a divine revelation and sacred books, even if these had become incomplete and obsolete. Pagans who fell under Islamic rule had to choose between conversion to Islam and death, whereas Jews and Christians still had the option of putting themselves under the protection of the state and paying the so-called poll tax (Arabic *jizyah*). In return, the state guaranteed their lives, their property, and their right to practice their own religion, though it imposed a number of restrictions and prohibitions intended to symbolize the subjection and degradation of non-Muslim minorities with respect to Muslims (for example, rules regarding clothing and prohibitions on riding horses and carrying weapons). The source for these regulations, which eventually developed into a complex system of prescriptions, were the past relationships between Muhammad and Jewish and Christian groups in other parts of Arabia and certain guiding principles announced in the form of revelations and later recorded in the Qur'an. Originally, only Jews and Christians, since they were expressly mentioned in Muhammad's revelations, were granted the status of "people of the book." After the conquest of Iran, Muslims also granted this status to adherents of Zoroastrianism, which was the state religion of Sasanian Iran, relying on a tradition according to which Muhammad was supposed to have accepted poll tax payments from Zoroastrians in Bahrain.

Therefore, in accord with the Prophet's practice, the Arabs generally did not force the peoples they conquered to convert to Islam; instead, they entered into agreements with them in return for payment of the poll tax. The Arabs ensured the progress of their conquests and their ongoing presence in the areas they conquered by building new garrison cities in the course of their military campaigns—cities such as Basra and Kufah in the southern part of present-day Iraq. Finally, in a second wave of campaigns at the beginning of the eighth century, Transoxania was conquered. By this point large numbers of Arabs had settled in almost every part of Iran and intermarried with the native population. Even today the Arab heritage of many Iranian tribes and families can still be traced.

In the territories the Muslims conquered real property was usually not taken away from its owners, but they had to pay a property tax (Arabic *kharaj*) if they did not convert to Islam. Only at the beginning of the eighth century, when the number of Muslims significantly increased, did the latter have to start paying this property tax as well in order to fill the state's coffers. Land that was left practically ownerless because the owners had died or fled was appropriated by the authorities and awarded to Arabs. Naturally, this was not always done in an orderly way; illegal appropriations of land and even unauthorized divvying-up of provinces—as in Kirman in southeast Iran—by Arabs also occurred. In rural areas the *dihqan* (landlord) played an important role after the conquest. Since the late Sasanian era these landlords had constituted a lower level of landed aristocrats who owned lands of a certain size and who were responsible for local administration. They maintained their land holdings by means of payments in cash or kind to individual Arab military leaders and often, to be sure, by converting to Islam. As was already the case under the Sasanian Empire, in the early Islamic period the dihqans were also responsible for collecting taxes as well as for cultivating the land and maintaining roads and bridges. Some dihqans were almost independent local rulers, particularly in Eastern Iran. Only at the end of the tenth century did this modest form of landed property gradually disappear, and along with it the importance of the dihqans.

The Arabs incorporated the whole Sasanian territory into their empire (which they had not done in the case of the Byzantine areas they had conquered), but they were not prepared to govern so enormous a territory. For that reason they adopted the Persian model of a self-contained imperial government and left the existing administrative apparatus untouched. Persian remained in use as the language of the chancellery, and began to be replaced by Arabic only toward the end of the seventh century as a result of a general Islamization of the administration. Similarly, the Arabs kept in place trained officials in various branches of the administration. This Persian bureaucracy, referred to in Arabic as *kuttab* (sing. *katib*, "scribe, secretary"), had extensive knowledge and experience that could only be of use to the Muslims. From the ranks of the *kuttâb* emerged numerous dig-

nitaries, statesmen, and literary figures who enjoyed complete mastery not only of their native tongues but also of
Arabic. It was the secretaries who, by keeping alive old Iranian traditions and combining their own spiritual world with
the new faith, made an important Iranian contribution to
the development of Islam and universal Islamic culture.
During the first Islamic century—from the reign of the first
four caliphs to the end of the Umayyad dynasty (600-749)—
a distinction was still drawn between Muslims who were of
Arab descent and those who were not, even though this was
incompatible with Islam's later egalitarian claim that all
Muslims, regardless of their ancestry, are equal. Muslims
who were not of Arab descent—and this included almost all
new converts—had to become the "clients" or "mawali"
(Arabic *mawali*) of an Arab tribe or prominent Arab individual. Even if they were wealthy and educated, they did not
enjoy all the rights of Arab Muslims, and their social standing was lower. Although *mawâlî* were of differing ethnic heritage, the majority of them were Iranians, and hence as a
whole the problem was an Iranian one. Therefore the mawali
felt a certain sympathy for other groups that were opposed
to Umayyad rule. The fourth caliph, ʿAli (656-661), with
whom the origin of the Shiʿite faith is connected, is said to
have made the mawali the equals of the Arabs, much to the
annoyance of the latter. In particular, the mawali living in
Kufah were among ʿAli's adherents. This explains the strong
early response that Shiʿism among Iranians, as well as the
fact that many Iranians participated in the Shiʿite rebellions
against the Umayyads, including for instance the one that
ultimately led to the Umayyads' fall in 749.

The Islamization of Iran

Although there were some local skirmishes, the Islamization of Iran was achieved largely without fighting. It took place over several centuries, continuing to advance slowly and gradually until the middle of the eighth century. It has occasionally been said that whole sections of the population converted to Islam, but this seems seldom to have been the case. However, it is difficult to determine exactly what was meant by a true conversion to Islam—whether, for instance, it was necessary to demonstrate that one was familiar with Islamic forms of worship and that one was able to read the Qur'an. Presumably many people converted formally to Islam without really knowing what duties were connected with being a Muslim; often enough, they have have given it no more than lip service. Moreover, depending on the region, Islamization proceeded in entirely different ways. In some provinces, such as Fars, Jibal, Gilan, and Daylam, most of the people initially kept their old religious beliefs. Some documents suggest that significant Zoroastrian minorities continued to exist in these areas well into the tenth century, and in southeast Iran the Zoroastrians' holy fire seems to have burned even into the thirteenth century. We can assume that much the same can be said for other areas of Iran; since Zoroastrians were recognized as "people of the book," they were able to go on practicing their religion without serious restrictions.

Conversion to Islam often depended on membership in a specific social group. For instance, tradesmen and workers in cities belonged to a group more open to conversion to

Islam than were farmers or the Zoroastrian priesthood. Craftsmen and workers were considered impure by the priests because their occupations inevitably led them to violate numerous Zoroastrian regulations, such as the taboo on polluting fire, water, and earth. Islam, which does not have these rigid regulations, therefore constituted an acceptable alternative. As in these cases, social or economic grounds may often have been crucial factors in the decision to convert to Islam. Many members of the Iranian upper class apparently converted quite rapidly in order to preserve their property, their social standing, or their fiscal privileges, to escape paying the poll tax, or to make it easier to join the new Muslim elite.

Although social and economic reasons played a far larger role than force employed by the conqueror, there was evidently no lack of missionary zeal and even coercion on the part of the Muslims, and this makes it only too clear that the conversion of many Iranians to Islam was at first merely superficial. It appears that the number of conversions to Islam sharply increased after the ʿAbbasids rose to power because they put Arabs and non-Arabs on the same level, thus eliminating the problem of the mawali. This must have significantly increased Iranians' willingness to adopt Islam. It may also be that there was already—as later historical sources indicate—a tendency to resist allowing non-Muslims to participate fully in community life or hold high political and social positions. The longer Muslim rule continued, the more the Islamization of Iran became an irreversible process that ultimately benefited the new religion. Nonetheless, the long survival of Zoroastrianism was manifested in the second half of the eighth and the first half of the ninth centuries in Iran, and especially in eastern Iran, by a series of syncretistic religious movements that combined elements of Zoroastrianism, Manichaeanism, and Mazdakism with Islamic ideas or expressed overt hostility to Islam; they were suppressed by the ʿAbbasid caliphs in Baghdad only with difficulty.

Shiʿism

Since the early modern period—and up to the present day—Iran has been a Shiʿite country. Shiʿism originated in the uncertainties that followed the death of the Prophet Muhammad. When the latter died in Medina in the summer of 632, he left behind no surviving male heir of his own, and had apparently established no rules regarding his succession. Thus the young Muslim community was forced to decide for itself who was to be the leader—that is, the caliph (from Arabic *khalifah*, "successor," "deputy," i.e., of the prophet Muhammad)—of the post-Prophet community. In determining the group of legitimate candidates for the leadership of the Muslim community, the genealogical principle played an important role, as did also early credit for spreading and supporting the new religion. In the end, family ties to the Prophet proved to be the decisive factor. It was this—only superficially political—question of the legitimacy of the caliph that resulted in the split between Sunnis and Shiʿites in the Muslim community that has persisted to the present day.

The term *Shiʿah* means "party" in the sense of faction. It refers to those contemporaries of the Prophet who sought, during the conflicts regarding succession that broke out after his death, to reserve the leadership of the community for 'Ali, Muhammad's cousin and son-in-law (he was married to the Prophet's daughter Fatima). Contrary to many popular Western and Sunni notions that often tend to equate Shi'ism with Iran and thus to suggest a historically doubtful opposition between an ethnically defined Arab Sunnism and an Iranian Shi'ism, Shi'ism is anything but a special Iranian variant of Islam. The origin of Shi'ism lay in intra-Islamic conflicts in the Arab milieu of Medina; shortly afterward it was further developed in the equally Arab city of Kufah in what is now southern Iraq.

However, after Muhammad's death the leading members of the community in Medina first chose, from their own ranks, his father-in-law, Abu Bakr, as caliph (reigned from 632 to 634). The second caliph, 'Umar (reigned 634-644), who was also one of the Prophet's fathers-in-law, was designated by Abu Bakr. The reign of the third caliph, Uthman (reigned 644-656), the Prophet's son-in-law, was chosen by an electoral committee. After Uthman was murdered by rebellious soldiers, 'Ali finally became the caliph (reigned 656-661). However, 'Ali's caliphate was disputed from the outset. Above all, Uthman's relatives from the Umayya clan did not recognize 'Ali as caliph, and they left Medina and moved to Syria. 'Ali, for his part, went to the garrison city of Kufah, where he had faithful supporters who helped him in his battle for the caliphate. The five years of 'Ali's reign, during which his supporters fought the Umayya clan's followers for power, and therefore Muslims battled members of their own religion, ended in a final schism of the Muslim community. In the summer of 657, at Siffin on the banks of the Euphrates, 'Ali's army and that of his rival Mu'awiyah, a cousin of the murdered caliph Uthman, met in battle. After weeks of fighting, it was decided to resolve the whole question of the rightful ruler by referring it to a panel of arbitrators whose deliberations were to be guided by the Qur'an. Reports regarding this panel are contradictory, so that the question about who had a legitimate right to the caliphate remains unanswered. In any case, 'Ali's agreement to abide by the arbitrators' decision proved fateful, since some of his supporters were angered by these events and deserted him. In their view, 'Ali had abdicated the caliphate that was rightfully his by making his claim to it subject to the decision of human judges. In 661, 'Ali was murdered by one of these dissidents (Arabic *khawarij*, "seceders"). The preceding year his rival Mu'awiyah had already proclaimed himself caliph in Jerusalem, thereby founding the Umayyad dynasty (661-749). The problem of the caliph's legitimacy had thus become a pure battle for power, even if it was conducted by means of religious arguments.

For the Shi'ites, the "party of 'Ali," 'Ali is the sole legitimate successor of the Prophet Muhammad as the leader of the Muslim community. 'Ali's close genealogical relationship to the Prophet spoke in his favor, and he was also among the first to convert to Islam. However, the Shi'ite's base 'Ali's claim to be the Prophet's immediate successor primarily on a series of traditions of which the most important is an utterance Muhammad is supposed to have made on his return from his last pilgrimage from Mecca to Medina in 632, the year of his death. On March 16—according to the

Muslim calendar, the eighteenth day of the pilgrimage
month Dhu al-Hijjah—the pilgrims were resting by the pool
of Khumm, halfway between the two cities. There Muhammad is supposed to have said, "Whoever accepts me as master (*mawla*), ʿAli is his master too." Shiʿites interpret this
statement as the Prophet's designation of ʿAli as his successor. For them, that day at the pool of Khumm has extraor-
dinary meaning, and from the tenth century on, it became
the second most important Shiʿite holiday and is still celebrated today. Sunnis also recognize this tradition, but they
consider it less important, and in any case they do not
regard it as an express command regarding the succession;
instead, they interpret it as merely expressing the Prophet's
desire to strengthen ʿAli's status within the community, in
which he had for various reasons made himself unpopular.

The first three caliphs, Abu Bakr, ʿUmar, and Uthman,
are not recognized by Shiʿism as legitimate rulers; they are
seen as having usurped a position that should by rights have
gone to ʿAli from the outset. For the Sunnis, in contrast, the
first four caliphs were all equally legitimate leaders of the
community and deserve the same respect, since according to
Sunnis the only requirement is that the caliph belong to the
Prophet's tribe, the Quraysh. Thus Sunnis and Shiʿites have
completely opposed views of the course of early Islamic history. The ferocity of the conflicts between the two groups,
which continues today, becomes comprehensible when we
consider that according to Islamic belief, a divine plan of
salvation underlies history, and that this plan culminates in
a final judgment day. Since in Islam the religious and secular communities are completely fused, the task set for the

community consists in making this divinely willed form of the state manifest in the temporal world, thereby fulfilling the divine plan so far as possible. This view gives political events their religious meaning, and it is the reason for the enormous importance of the question regarding the legitimate caliph: only a legitimate leader of the Muslim community can guide it through worldly life in accord with God's will. According to Shi'ism, the Sunnis, who did not support 'Ali's claim to the caliphate, disregarded God's will and thereby committed a grave sin. In the Shi'ite view, the history of the early Muslim community did not unfold in accord with God's will, and since it cannot be undone, the Sunnis can in principle never atone for the sin they committed against 'Ali.

At the present time, about 10 to 15 percent of all Muslims worldwide adhere to Shi'ism in one form or another. The most important and numerically largest group among these is "Twelver Shi'ism" (*Ithna 'Ashariyyah*), the current state religion of Iran.

The Doctrine of Twelver Shi'ism

Regarding the question which of 'Ali's descendants had the right to lead the Muslim community after his death in 661, the views of the various Shi'ite factions differ. For Twelver Shi'ism, only 'Ali's descendants from his first marriage with the Prophet's daughter Fatima count as legitimate. The term "Twelver" is derived from the number of the leaders of the Muslim community considered legitimate, beginning with 'Ali himself. Twelver Shi'ites are also called "imamites," after the title "imam" ("leader or head of the community") accorded to ʿAli and his successors. A third name for the Twelver Shiʿites is "Jaʿfariyyah," after the sixth Imam, Jaʿfar (d. 765), who played an especially important role in shaping the Twelver Shiʿites' doctrine.

The Twelvers' eleventh imam was not yet thirty when he died (sometime between 873 and 874) without—according to the general tradition—having left a male heir. At this point the unresolved question of who was his legitimate successor as the community's new imam divided the imamites into various sects and factions. However, one of these groups had from the outset disputed the notion that the eleventh imam had left no heir, maintaining that he had a young son born in 869, and that it was no accident that his name was Muhammad, like the Prophet's. Through a miracle, they claimed, this Muhammad had gone into occultation. Since then, he is supposed to have resided somewhere in the world, invisible , hidden. One day, no one knows when, the hidden twelfth imam is expected to return. His is called al-Mahdi ("divinely guided one") and he will return as a redeemer after a series of heavenly signs; it is for him to complete the Prophet's task, to overthrow the rule of usurpers and tyrants, and to establish the realm of justice, a paradise on Earth. This belief in the existence of a hidden twelfth imam and his future return became the most important characteristic of Twelver Shiʿism.

Twelver Shiʿism was given its special religious imprint by the fate of ʿAli's younger son Husayn, the third imam. When the Umayyad caliph Muʿawiyah died in Damascus in 680 and the son he had named as his heir, Yazid, succeeded him,

Husayn attempted to take over the caliphate by force of arms. Relying on his supporters in Kufah, he invaded Iraq along with a small group of faithful followers from Medina. However, the help he expected to receive from the Shi'ites in Kufah was not forthcoming, and his troops were almost wiped out in a battle fought on October 10, 680 (according to the Muslim calendar, on the tenth day of Muharram in the year 61) near the little town of Karbala, some 70 kilometers north of Kufah. The day of this battle, known as "'Ashura" ("the tenth," i.e., the tenth day of Muharram) signifies both Shi'ism's political failure and the true beginning of Shi'ite religious feeling. With the defeat at Karbala, Shi'ism was politically played out, and for centuries it was merely a movement opposing Sunni rule. However, it was only after Karbala that Twelver Shi'ism developed its typical religious rituals of penitence and mourning. For Twelvers, the day of Karbala is the day of Husayn's martyrdom, which he suffered blamelessly. On this day—'Ashura—and the nine days preceding it in the month of Muharram, Twelvers commemorate his death. The rituals carried out on this occasion, which outsiders often see as mere expressions of mourning, are far more than that: they are rituals of penitence, through which the believer seeks to atone for his own guilt with regard to the fate of the third imam. The origin of this is apparently the feeling of the Shi'ite supporters in Kufah that at Karbala they had left Husayn in the lurch. In the fall of 684, a group of "penitents" left Kufah for Karbala in order to sacrifice themselves. The participants in this effort were in fact almost all killed by Umayyad troops at the beginning of January, 685. The acceptance of self-sacrifice, together with lamentation over the fate of the imam, is still today the most prominent mark of Twelver religious feeling.

According to Twelver tradition, not only Husayn but all the other imams—except for the twelfth—died a violent death: they were murdered by their enemies or perished in the latter's dungeons. Like Husayn, they had all innocently suffered and are therefore regarded as martyrs, just as he is, and Shi'ites celebrate the days of their martyrdom as holidays, with the sole exception of the twelfth imam, whose birthday is celebrated. The graves of the first eleven imams are greatly venerated by believers and are the goals of many Shi'ite pilgrimages. The Muharram celebrations, which are attested as early as the tenth century, at first included publicly performed songs of lamentation and processions. Starting in the seventeenth century, European travelers reported bloody processions of flagellants that sometimes degenerated into street fighting in the course of which people were killed. Finally, among the characteristic customs of Muharram celebrations are dramatic representations of the events in Karbala—so-called "passion plays" (ta'ziyeh, "expressions of mourning") performed in public.

Processions of flagellants during the month of Muharram, which are often regarded with mistrust by Shi'ite theologians and sometimes prohibited by the authorities, are now common everywhere in Iran. The excited atmosphere during these occasions, on which thousands of believers come together, has proven to be politically explosive right down to the present day. The story of Husayn and his opponent Yazid can easily be given a contemporary context whenever it is a question of protesting what is seen as a tyrannical or unjust government. How effectively the events of early Islamic history can be instrumentalized politically has been impressively shown by the 1979 Islamic Revolution in Iran.

According to their own conception, Twelver Shi'ites have lived under what they consider legitimate rule only once: during the five years of 'Ali's caliphate. None of the imams following him ever succeeded in taking power again, the Shi'ite community has ever since lived under authorities it considers illegitimate. Moreover, after the concealment of the twelfth imam the Twelvers have remained entirely without leadership, for only the returned twelfth imam can be their legitimate leader. Even in seclusion he is the sole legitimate authority for Twelver Shi'ites, so that until he returns no earthly power can enjoy more than a temporary and strictly limited legitimacy. The problem that confronted the Shi'ites was who could rightfully lead them while they awaited the return of the hidden imam. After many disputes, this task was finally assigned to the Shi'ite scholars. The most current formulation of the principle that only this group, as representatives of the hidden imam, are allowed to lead the Shi'ite community, is found in the Ayatollah Khomeini's doctrine of the "representative governance by the jurist" (in Persian, *vilayat-i faqih*). The representative ruling power of the Shi'ite scholars during the absence of the twelfth imam is also established in the Islamic Republic's constitution.

The ʿAbbasid Caliphate

The ʿAbbasid dynasty (750-1258) traced its lineage back to al-ʿAbbas, an uncle of the Prophet's. As members of Muhammad's family, they were in the Sunnis' opinion legitimate rulers, from a religious point of view. The ʿAbbasids had promoted the fall of the Umayyads by means of clandestine propaganda they entrusted to Abu Muslim, one of their freedmen of Iranian descent. Officially, Abu Muslim supported a pretender from the Quraysh clan of Hashim, which was Muhammad's and ʿAli's clan, thereby gaining the support of Shiʿites. However, Abu Muslim was for an imam whom he named only indirectly as "the one from Muhammad's house who wins approval." The center of his propaganda efforts was in Marv, in Khurasan, where Arabs had settled in great numbers with their *mawali*, in order to continue Muslim expansion toward Inner Asia. Starting in 747, at the head of his rebel army Abu Muslim conquered eastern Iran and then drove westward, where he took Kufah in 749. There Abu al-ʿAbbas, a member of the ʿAbbasid family, suddenly emerged and had himself honored as caliph; the overthrow of the Umayyads by ʿAbbasid troops came soon afterward. The Shiʿites, who had wanted to fight to win the caliphate for one of ʿAli's descendants, were now forced to recognize that they had helped a new usurper take power. It is clear that the Shiʿites, deprived of their hopes, saw the ʿAbbasids' action as a betrayal.

The ʿAbbasids followed the Prophet's original idea and abolished the clientele relationship. By making Arab and non-Arab Muslims legally equal, the Islamic state acquired a cosmopolitan character. The "Arabian Empire" of the Umayyads, as it is often called because of the privilege it accorded Arabs, was transformed into an "Islamic Empire" in which the concept of the *mawali* eventually became obsolete and in the ninth century disappeared entirely. Only then did the old culture of the Near East, whose traditions were transmitted by non-Arabs who had gone over to Islam, fuse with the new Islamic religion. Pre-Islamic Iranian ideas must have played a major role in this process.

In order to escape the Shi'ite milieu of Kufah, the caliph al-Mansur (reigned 754-775) founded in 762 the city of Baghdad in present-day Iraq, which remained—with a short interuption in the ninth century—the residence of the 'Abbasid caliphs until it was taken by the Mongols in 1258,. The choice of a site near the ancient Sasanian capital of Ctesiphon (Arabic *al-Mada'in*, lit. "cities") and the city's layout make the shaping influence of pre-Islamic Iranian concepts of power clear.Baghdad is a remarkable example of purposeful city-planning. It was laid out as a round city, resembling a fortress with its three concentric walls; the caliph's palace, the main mosque, and the state administration were all inside the innermost wall. The city had four gates and was divided into four districts of equal size that could be closed off and guarded during the night. This round city, praised by Arab chroniclers as unique, and of which nothing has survived, was probably modeled on the round city layouts of the ancient Near East; we know of several round or oval layouts for cities dating from the age of the Sasanians, including Ctesiphon itself. The separation of the caliph from the people, which al-Mansur's Baghdad

makes visible, along with the ruler's ability to exercise surveillance over his subjects at all times, correspond entirely to
the position of an ancient Sasanian Great King. The administration was also obviously modeled on Sasanian institutions: religious, civil, and military responsibilities, which
under the Umayyads had been vested in one person, were
now separated and a supreme administrative official, the
vizier, was introduced; he was the caliph's direct subordinate.
Often it was officials of Iranian descent who rose to high
administrative positions and even to the post of vizier.
Ancient Persian notions of royal splendor may also have
influenced the sumptuous character of life at the ʿAbbasid
court, with its magnificent buildings, opulent banquets, and
varied courtly ceremonies. The caliphs celebrated Iranian
holidays, especially the spring festival of Noruz, and they
enjoyed playing polo, one of the ancient Persians' favorite
sports. All this, together with a high regard for Iranian
craftsmanship, gave the culture of the ʿAbbasidian court a
distinctly Persian appearance.

Militarily the ʿAbbasids no longer relied, as had the
Umayyads, on Arab tribal fighters, but instead, to an increasing extent, on soldiers recruited from Khurasan. The
caliph al-Muʿtasim (reigned 833-842) created a bodyguard
that was under his direct command and was composed of
military slaves, chiefly of Turkish descent, who were bought
on the steppes of Inner Asia when they were still children
and raised as soldiers. They constituted the heart of the
ʿAbbasidian army. However, this quickly proved to be a fateful step: instead of being a militarily effective instrument in
the hands of the caliph, these guards increasingly gained

political power. Frequent encroachments by the Turks, which al-Mu'tasim was unable to keep under control, on the people of Baghdad led to fighting in the streets and revealed the caliph's military weakness with regard to his army. The removal in 836 of the imperial residence to the newly founded garrison city of Samarra in northern Iraq was not to be a long-term solution; in 892 the 'Abbasid court returned to Baghdad because a similar intolerable situation had developed in Samarra. The Turkish guards installed and overthrew the caliphs at will, so that by the ninth century the caliphate lost all real political power. The authority of the caliphs was no more than a fiction maintained for the benefit of outsiders, whereas the caliphate itself now represented only ideally the vanished unity of the Muslim universal community. Under these circumstances, independent territorial rulers began to appear as early as the beginning of the ninth century, at first on the periphery of the empire, and then also in its core lands, so that the actual territory controlled by the caliphate finally shrank to the immediate environs of Baghdad. However, many of the new dynasties had their rule confirmed by the caliph and thereby religiously justified, so that at least in theory the unity of the caliphate was preserved.

In 945, finally, the imperial residence of Baghdad was itself conquered by the Buyids, a mountain people from northern Iran. The Buyids "liberated" the 'Abbasids from their Turkish guards, but they also seized political power for themselves, leaving the caliph only his moral authority. In 1055, the Saljuqs succeeded the Buyids, and ruled just as independently. After a short revival of the caliphate in the twelfth century, it was overthrown by the Mongols, the successors of Genghis Khan, in 1258, when they sacked Baghdad and killed the last ʿAbbasid caliph.

The Samanids

Starting in the first half of the ninth century, following the disintegration of the vast ʿAbbasid Empire, dynasties came to power in Iran that ruled de facto autonomously, even if—like many others—they nominally supported the caliph and made no claim to his title. Here, on the eastern edge of the caliphate, pre-Islamic Iranian traditions had remained alive that –now associated with the religion of Islam—shaped Iran's new cultural independence within the Islamic community and also gave Islam itself a new direction.

After the Tahirids (821-873), the earliest autonomous dynasty in Iran, which ruled the province of Khurasan practically independently, and after the Saffarids (867-903), who created a short-lived but enormous empire extending from Kabul in present-day Afghanistan to Isfahan, the Samanids (892-999) established in Transoxania, the caliphate's frontier province, a stable rule that they then extended to Khurasan. Their ancestor Saman—who lived in the eighth century—is supposed to have been a dihqan. According to the unanimous testimony of Muslim chroniclers he had fled, for unknown reasons, to Khurasan, where he converted to Sunni Islam. As a reward for their faithful service, the Caliph named Saman's grandsons to various gubernatorial positions in Transoxania. Under Ismaʿil (reigned 892-907), the true founder of Samanid rule, an empire emerged that was de facto independent of the caliphate and was at that time the greatest power in the Islamic East. In their capital, Bukhara, the Samanids created a centralized administration modeled on the caliph's court that became in turn a model for the Saljuqs and other dynasties: the ruler appointed provincial governors who were responsible for collecting taxes and were required to provide troops when needed. Militarily, the Samanids succeeded in making their territory safe for Sunni Islam by protecting it against attacks by the pagan Turks of the steppes of Inner Asia. Like the Tahirids before them, the Samanids imported Turkish military slaves into the caliphate's lands, but no longer for the caliph's court alone. Since its beginning under al-Muʿtasim, military slavery had developed into the basis of the army, so that the need—together with the price—had significantly increased. This profitable business, coupled with a prudent encouragement of trade to which the spread of Samanid coins as far as Scandinavia and the Rhine testifies, led to greater economic prosperity.

The Samanids turned their residence in Bukhara into a cosmopolitan center of artistic and intellectual creation that was also the center of what is often called the "Iranian Renaissance." Their own affinity with the Iranian past is shown in the old Persian title *shahanshah* ("king of kings") that they bore, and in their claim to be descended from the Sasanian military commander and later Great King Bahram Chubin (ruled 590-591). At their court, the Samanid rulers generously promoted New Persian language and poetry. The language of the court was Persian, which may at this early date have already been used alongside Arabic in the administration. In Samanid Bukhara a revival of pre-Islamic Iranian traditions took place that should not, however, be misunderstood as a mere return to the past, as is suggested by the term "Renaissance," and certainly not as a reaction of an Iranian national consciousness to Arab Islam. Instead, the return to old Iranian traditions occurred in combination with Islam, so that we might more properly speak of an Islamic-Iranian Renaissance. It was the Samanids' achievement to have shown that Islam as a religion, and above all as a culture, need not remain bound to the Arabic language. By separating it from its purely Arab background, they freed it from the narrow, Bedouin conditions in which it had originated. They showed the way to make the new religion more flexible and adaptable than it had earlier been, and to ensure that it would have a future beyond the Arabs. Just as the Samanids had combined their own—Old Persian—tradition with Islam, other peoples could do the same in the future. Thus Islam became a truly universal religion and culture, open to all people.

The Samanids were the last dynasty of Iranian descent in Transoxania. Their decline and fall had many causes. Internal rebellions weakened the empire; the Turkish military slaves who made up the Samanid army seized power, as they had already done in Baghdad. Finally, Khurasan fell to the Turkish Ghaznavid dynasty (977-1186), which invaded the province from eastern Afghanistan, while Transoxania fell to the Turkish QaraKhanid dynasty (992-1212), which advanced from the north. Only one architectural testimony to the artistically brilliant Samanid age is still extant in Bukhara: the mausoleum of the founder of the dynasty,

Ismaʿil. This is a four-arched edifice built on the model of Sasanian fire-temples and completely covered with tiles in which patterns were inscribed with great craftsmanship; it is one of the great masterpieces of Islamic architecture.

The Buyids

The family of the Buyids (Arabized as "Buwayhids"), who took their name from their ancestor Buyeh, came from the Daylam region on the southern coast of the Caspian Sea. In this mountainous area Islam established itself only relatively late. The inhabitants of Daylam were known as courageous foot soldiers; they had fought in the Caucasus as the Sasanians' allies and more than once repelled Muslim attacks on their homeland before in the ninth century they gradually began to open up to Islam, which was spread in Daylam chiefly by Shiʿite groups. The Buyids, like most of the people of Daylam, belonged to the Zaydiyyah, a moderate Shiʿite branch that considers the succession of imams after Husayn to be still open and does not believe in a hidden imam. However, they especially encouraged the Twelvers, probably under the influence of their viziers. Like the Turks, the people of Daylam had already served as mercenaries before the reign of the Buyids, and Buyeh's three sons—Ali, Hasan, and Ahmad—also began their careers in the army of Mardaviz (reigned 931-935), who came from the Daylamite clan of the Ziyarids and had brought the greater part of northern Iran under his rule. After Mardaviz was murdered by his Turkish mercenaries in 935, his short-lived kingdom rapidly fell apart. In only a few years the three

brothers of the Buyid family had established their control
over central and western Iran and Mesopotamia, which they
were to rule for over a century (945-1055). In 945, Ahmad
took Baghdad and made himself the caliph's "protector."

The third Buyid ruler, ʿAdud al-Dawlah (reigned 978-983)
united all the Buyid territories in Iraq, Iran, and Oman. As
a result, the center of power—at least after the fall of the
Samanids—was shifted to western Iran, the area of the former Sasanian Empire. Like the Samanids before them, the
Buyids assumed the old Persian title of *shahanshah* ("king of
kings"); Adud ad-Daula had himself formally crowned as
king by the caliph, and it is no surprise that he now also
claimed to be descended from the Sasanian emperor Bahram Gur (reigned 421-439). Although in the meantime many
Iranians had gone over to Islam, and Adud ad-Daula considered himself a devout Muslim, the pre-Islamic idea of
kingship was—in parallel with the "Iranian Renaissance" in
eastern Iran—still important in the west.

From a religious point of view, the Buyids were in no way
legitimate rulers, so that they urgently needed the Sunni
caliphate, especially since the large majority of their subjects
were Sunnis. In addition to their old Persian title the Buyids
therefore assumed the already existing title of commander-
in-chief (*amir al-ʿUmara*). In the Buyids the Shiʿah nonetheless found powerful protectors and promoters. Under the
first Buyid ruler, Ahmad, the main Shiʿite holidays—
ʿAshura and the commemoration of ʿAli's designation at the
pool of Khumm—were for the first time publicly celebrated.
The Buyids frequently made pilgrimages to the graves of the
Shiʿite imams, whose shrines they enlarged and surrounded

with walls to protect them from Bedouin attacks. ʿAli's and Fatimah's many descendants received privileges such as annual pensions or payments made from revenue derived from pious donations if they could prove the authenticity of their descent. A special office of the *naqib al-ashraf* ("marshal of the nobility") was set up, presumably in the ninth century, to record and verify genealogical connections with ʿAli's family. Insofar as the descendants of ʿAli and Fatima—who were allowed to use the titles *sharif* ("noble," for the descendants of ʿAli's son Hasan) and *sayyid* ("lord," for the descendants of ʿAli's son Husayn)—developed into a kind of religious aristocracy, the office of *naqib al-ashraf* also acquired social prestige. During the Buyid dynasty the standard canonical books distinguishing the Twelvers' religious doctrine and law from those of other Shiʿite denominations appeared, about a century after the corresponding Sunni books were written. It is moreover interesting to note that the authors of the canonical works of the Buyid period already made Shiʿite scholars, as representatives of the twelfth imam, responsible for leading the Shiʿite community. Although the scholars' representative leadership of the Shiʿite community long remained in dispute, the direction it would take is already foreshadowed here.

From the outset the Buyids had no established regulation regarding succession to the throne; usually, various branches of the family ruled in the cities and provinces of Iran and Iraq unless an energetic personality like Adud ad-Daula was able to gain their general support. However, this political fragmentation benefited the various seats of government— such as the cities of Rayy, Isfahan, and Shiraz—whose rulers erected splendid edifices and were active as patrons and promoters of the arts. The frequent internal conflicts between the later Buyids made it easier for their opponents to take one province after another away from them. In 1055 the Saljuqs conquered Baghdad, and thereafter the Buyids continued to rule only in Fars, until this province also fell to the Saljuqs.

The Continuing Existence of Iranian Traditions

The Islamic civilization of the Middle Ages, as it developed under the ʿAbbasids, may initially appear to outsiders to be an Arabian culture, because of the dominance of Arabic as the language of the Qurʾan, science, and literature, but its content has in fact been essentially shaped by Iranian culture. Scholars and men of letters of Iranian descent, many of whom came from bureaucratic families, concerned themselves with the pre-Islamic past of Iran, which they sought to harmonize with their own time and with the religion of Islam. In the eighth century, Iranian Muslims started producing numerous translations of Sasanian court literature from Middle Persian into Arabic, and thereby introduced Iranian historical traditions into the Muslim view of history. The dominant model of this Persian tradition of rulership and the statecraft was the empire of the Sasanians, who had amalgamated the Persian past with their own dynasty to produce a more or less official view of history. The latter was expressed in the Middle Persian "Book of Kings" (*Khoday-Namak*), composed under the rule of Khusraw Parviz (reigned 590-628). This work compiled mythical, legendary, and historical material and provided a chronological history of Iran beginning with the first king, Gayomart. The translation of this work into Arabic by the Iranian state secretary Ibn al-Muqaffa (d. 757) made this self-image of the Sasanian kings known to the educated Muslim world. The Sasanian Empire thus became the standard model of the traditional conception of state rulership and thinking in connection with pre-Islamic Persia.

During the period of governmental and social reorientation under the first ʿAbbasid caliphs, a new literary genre emerged that was concerned with statecraft and became a favorite vehicle for the expression of Islamic-Iranian traditions of rulership: the "mirror for princes," which was addressed with admonitory intention to kings and rulers and that sought to instruct them regarding the ethical and moral principles of government. Since the subjects these works dealt with did not exist in the original Islamic tradition, their authors were from the outset Iranian Muslims, even if they wrote at first in Arabic, and only later, at the beginning of the tenth century, in New Persian. However, these authors provided the traditional concept of the king with new traits in order to adapt it to the Islamic religion. The mirrors for princes thus clearly testify to the consciousness of political and cultural continuity that motivated their Iranian authors, and are at the same time our most important source of information regarding the development of the image of Iran in the Islamic age.

A basic feature of the Persian conception of the ruler was the doctrine of charisma, *khvarnah*, the possession of which distinguished the king from other men and legitimated him.

Charisma was seen as a light that radiated from the ruler; hence its Arabic translation as *nur*, "light." God gave the Persian king the gift of wisdom, and this enabled him to exercise justice and do good. The king acted on behalf of God, and just as God ruled over the heavenly sphere, so did the king rule over the earthly sphere. The equivalent juxtaposition of prophet and king, of the Islamic and non-Islamic, in the mirrors for princes—a juxtaposition that is of course entirely impermissible from a theological point of view—necessarily led to many reinterpretations of the Iranian idea of rulership that made it compatible with the Islamic conception of rulership which demanded that the caliph be in immediate contact with his subjects. The absolute ruler thus became—according to the traditional model of the first four caliphs, to whom this attribute was ascribed —a king who was close to his people and always available to them. The Iranian ruler's throne, which was originally a symbol of his distance from the people, was interpreted in the mirrors for princes as a means of giving the king a better overview during audiences.

The Persian monarchical tradition remained alive in the history of Iran down to the modern period. Under the Qajar rulers of the nineteenth century, for instance, the "chest of justice" that was sent to the provinces so that even subjects living in the most remote parts of the country might send their petitions to the capital symbolized the accessibility of the rulers. In the twentieth century, the Pahlavis repeatedly invoked old Iranian ideas that could in case of need be visually represented: thus during the coronation ceremonies in 1967, the crown and the Qur'an were presented to the Shah by two soldiers walking side by side—the Iranian idea of the state and Islam symbolically appearing as completely equal in importance.

The Beginnings of New Persian Literature

Persian belongs to the Indo-Iranian (Aryan) group of the Indo-European family of languages. In the first centuries after the fall of the Sasanian Empire, the official language of which had been Middle Persian, or so-called Pahlavi, New Persian developed and was henceforth written in Arabic script. Thereby it constituted the basis for a peculiarly Iranian cultural development that in the course of its later history put its stamp on large geographical areas reaching as far as the Near East, Central Asia, and India.

The first examples of New Persian literature appeared in the east, far from the center of the caliphate, and until the tenth century they were limited to Transoxania and Khurasan. There, without strong competition from other languages, New Persian could more freely develop as a literary medium. As sparse early reports suggest, New Persian was at first used in courtly poetry addressed to local potentates, princes, and dignitaries. Many of these understood little Arabic or none at all, so that poets had to compose their panegyrics in New Persian, which was widely understood. Except for a few examples, early poetry in New Persian has been lost; the oldest poetic fragments extant go back only as far as the ninth century, complete poems to the tenth century. The most impressive figure among the early New Persian poets is the blind singer Rudaki (d. 940 or 950), who was active at the court of the Samanids and whose works are also extant only in fragments. According to the unanimous judgment of his contemporaries, his verse was regarded as the inimitable model of poetic language, so that he is often considered the father of Persian poetry. In addition to poetry, prose works were also written before the eleventh century in New Persian, among them books on geography, the exegesis of the Qur'an, and medicine, but few of these have survived. At the court of the Samanids, the vizier Abu Ali Bal'ami wrote a history of Iran (completed in 963), which he took from the annals—composed in Arabic—of al-Tabari (d. 923), who was also an author of Iranian descent, and reworked or expanded here and there. It is still the oldest known prose work in New Persian and until the time of the Mongols it remained the standard book on the history of Iran.

The Persian epic is a unique Iranian creation that grew out of the pre-Islamic royal tradition. Among the numerous epics in New Persian literature, there is basically only one outstanding heroic epic, which is often called the Iranian "national epic," though it also contains many romance-like elements: Ferdowsi's *Shahnameh*. Ferdowsi (d. after 1020) came from a wealthy dihqan family in Tus (modern Mashhad) in Khurasan. His *Shahnameh* (completed in 1010), which is more than 50,000 verses long, is a monumental epic on the early, pre-Islamic history of Iran that goes back into distant, mythical ages, and concludes in the age of the Sasanians. It weaves historical events and legends together. In this way it became a compendium of the Iranian heritage that provides an all-encompassing history of pre-Islamic

Iran and presents all the numerous kings and heroes constantly encountered in later Iranian literature. In the early
twentieth century, Iranian nationalists rediscovered Ferdowsi as the "re-awakener" of a particular Iranian identity
(after the Arab conquest of Iran in the seventh century) and
the *Shahnameh* as the literary monument of this identity.

CHAPTER II

Iran under the
Turks and Mongols
(1055-1501)

Turkish warrior

The Eleventh Century

In many respects, the eleventh century represents a significant turning-point in the history of Iran and of large parts of the Islamic world. From then on, and for many centuries, dynasties of Iranian descent were displaced by Turkish dynasties. Thus ended the "Iranian interlude," as scholars came to refer to the ninth and tenth centuries—the era of the Tahirids, the Safarids, the Samanids, and the Buyids. Although for a long time Turks had already played an important role in the armies of the caliphate and its provinces, up to that point they had been individuals separated from their former tribe or clan. Now, however, wave after wave of Turkish tribes from Central Asia began to migrate toward the west, streaming into the Islamic world and founding their own states and dynasties. Where Turks settled permanently, they changed the character of the country. The ethnic and linguistic layering of various peoples is visible in the spread of Turkish and Turkish-derived place names in the areas particularly favored by Turkish settlers. Turkish peoples appeared as advocates and defenders of Sunni Islam; after the end of the Buyid dynasty, Twelver Shi'ites were eliminated as a political force almost everywhere for the next five centuries. Despite the Turks' military ability, most of the states they founded proved to be relatively unstable; because of the lack of a fixed order of succession and the idea that subjected territory "belonged" not to the ruler alone but to his whole clan, sooner or later they disintegrated into various small regional states—an almost inevitable consequence of the battles over succession that regularly occurred when a sovereign died. This process took place repeatedly in Iran from the eleventh century on, until at the beginning of the sixteenth century the Safavid dynasty once again welded the various regional states into a single empire.

Originally, the Turks of Central Asia were nomads, but—unlike the Arab conquerors of Iran—they had very robust animals for riding and carrying loads. The Bactrian camel can endure cold and climb high mountains. Thus the advance of the Turks also spread their own way of life: nomadism. Unlike in Europe, where the role it played was small or non-existent, nomadism was an important factor shaping the Middle East. From that point on, relationships between nomads and sedentary peoples were marked by constant conflicts that led to devastation and a long-term decline of agriculture. To a large extent, climatic conditions determined the direction taken by the spread of the Turks, since for their animals they needed cool mountain meadows in the summer and mild lowland plains in the winter, moving back and forth semi-annually between the two. Thus, for instance, Azerbaijan in northwest Iran became one of the natural Turkish settlement areas.

The processes of change described above began on a large

scale under the Saljuqs (1040-1194), but the Turkish dynasty of the Ghaznavids (977-1186) was in many ways already typical of the new situation. Its founder was a military slave in the Samanid army who had risen to a high position and had brought a small territory in Ghazna (in modern Afghanistan) under his rule. The greatest ruler of the dynasty, Mahmud (reigned. 998-1030), was a devout Sunni who regarded himself as the defender of the caliph in Baghdad against inimical Shi'ite activities. He conquered a large empire that included Afghanistan, Khurasan, Khwarazm, and parts of northern India. Since it was essentially tailored to him as an individual, under his successor his empire was quickly lost to the Saljuqs, but the Ghaznavids held on in eastern Afghanistan and northern India for about a hundred and thirty years. The short-lived Ghaznavid Empire is the first example showing how the Turks from the steppes of Central Asia who came into contact with the high civilization of Iran claimed it as their own. On the military basis provided by the Turks, the court and the administration were organized on the Iranian model of the Samanids, while the official language of government remained Arabic. Despite their Turkish descent, the Ghaznavids bestowed upon themselves a genealogy that went back to a daughter of the last Sasanian king, Yazdgard III (reigned 633-651). The Ghaznavids, and especially Mahmud, enthusiastically supported and promoted Iranian culture and literature, as had the Samanids. Mahmud sought to emulate the already waning splendor of the Samanid court in Bukhara. He made his court in Ghazna into a widely known cultural center that attracted many scholars and poets.

From the Saljuqs to the Khwarazm-Shahs

The Saljuqs, who traced their name back to their ancestor Saljuq, were originally the leading family of a clan belonging to the Turkish tribal confederation of the Oghuz (Arabic *Ghuzz*) that lived during the tenth century on the steppes north of the Aral Sea and the Caspian Sea. Toward the end of the century, they converted to Islam, which had been spread in these regions on the frontiers of civilization chiefly by merchants and wandering preachers. After a crushing victory over Ghaznavid troops in 1040, near Dandanqan (between Marv and Sarakhs) in present-day Turkmenistan, the Saljuqs moved farther west and conquered the lands ruled by the Buyid family. In 1055, their leader Toghril Beg took Baghdad and thus ended the 110-year-long Shi'ite domination over the Sunni caliphate. As devout Sunnis, the Saljuqs revived the religious war, seeing themselves as holy warriors (Arabic *ghazi*) for orthodox Islam, which they sought not only to defend against heterodox denominations within the Islamic world, but also to spread to heretofore non-Islamic areas. The Saljuq Empire achieved its greatest extent under Malik-Shah (reigned 1073-1092). In 1071, he defeated the Byzantine emperor Romanos Diogenes (reigned 1068-1071) at Manzikert (now Malazgird, north of Lake Van in present-day Turkey), with the result that the enormous area between Anatolia and Transoxania now fell—at least nominally—under Saljuq rule.

Shortly after Malik-Shah's death, the Saljuq Empire collapsed into various regional powers. The situation remained relatively ordered and stable only in Transoxania, during the long rule of Malik-Shah's son Sanjar (reigned 1097-1157). The Saljuq Empire's tendency to disintegrate into smaller and smaller powers was promoted by the custom of appointing an Atabeg (Turkish "Prince Father") as tutor to the Saljuq princes who were given a province to govern. The Atabegs were Turkish military leaders who had their own following, who ruled with increasing independence, and who deprived their pupils of power and secured rulership for their own descendants. From the twelfth century, Atabeg dynasties ruled autonomously in various parts of Iran: in Shiraz, the Salghurids (1148-1282), in Tabriz, the Eldiguzids (1145-1225), and in Maragheh the Ahmadilis (1122-after 1220). Other Atabeg dynasties and local rulers from various branches of the Saljuq family composed a patchwork of new small states that ultimately reached across the whole of the Near East as far as Central Anatolia. At the beginning of the thirteenth century, the many Saljuq regional rulers were eliminated by the Khwarazm-Shahs (1077-1231), who conquered a large but very short-lived empire that extended from the boundaries of Anatolia to those of India. They started out from the remote Khwarezm oasis south of the Aral Sea. A governor installed there by Malik-Shah had bequeathed his office to his own descendants, who in turn took the title "Khwarazm-Shah" ("Ruler of Khwarezm"). Their empire, which was established at the beginning of the thirteenth century, soon fell victim to the Mongols led by Genghis Khan.

The Saljuq State

Like the Buyids before them, the Saljuqs, who had no religious legitimation, had their rule confirmed by the caliph. The latter granted their founder, Toghril Beg, various titles, including that of Sultan (Arabic *sultân,* lit. "power," "rule"). In earlier times some princes had used this title informally; now, however, it became an official title designating the independent—and usually Sunni—ruler of a territory. Characteristic of the Saljuq period was the dichotomy of caliph and sultan, which referred to two de facto separate spheres of authority. Whereas the caliph was now only the supreme religious and moral authority of the Muslim community, the sultan combined in his person the real political and military power. This new dichotomy, which was alien to the original Muslim conception of the state, actually only made the caliph's long-standing weakness more obvious.

For the government of their empire the Saljuqs adopted the traditional Iranian-Islamic institutions. Whereas the court offices responsible for organizing ceremonies and receptions were chiefly occupied by Turkish military leaders, the civil administration, with its numerous departments, remained in the hands of Iranian officials, who usually came from the bureaucratic class. Under the Saljuqs the vizier, as the highest civil official, was a very influential and powerful figure; he controlled the financial and fiscal department, the ruler's correspondence, and the military department, which was responsible for recruiting and paying soldiers and for maintaining the army. One of these viziers, Nizam al-Mulk, who held this office for thirty years under the sultans Alp

Arslan (reigned 1063-1072) and Malik-Shah (reigned 1073-1092), composed the *Siyasat-nameh* ("Book of Government"), which is one of the most important Persian prose works both because of its historical and cultural content and because of its outstanding language and style. Although during their campaigns of conquest the Saljuqs had relied on the support of their warlike nomadic hordes, once they took power they quickly replaced these troops with an army composed of military slaves and mercenaries. Nonetheless, familial bonds between the sultan and the tribes continued to exist. On the other hand, the Saljuqs were never able to find a satisfactory solution for the problem of integrating the nomadic tribes and their herds into the economy and society of Iran's sedentary population. Because additional Turkish groups were constantly emigrating from the steppes into Iran, and especially into Khurasan, the number of nomads steadily increased. However, the damage done to Iranian agriculture by these nomads was at first kept within limits—unlike what happened later on under the Mongols. Although many Turks remained in Iran, others moved westward in great numbers, where they found—in the Caucasus, Anatolia, and Syria—ample opportunities to fight for Islam. As a result of these migrations the number of nomads markedly increased in various areas of Iran where the climate suited them.

In order to meet the material demands of an excessively powerful army, the Buyids had already begun rewarding leading military figures by assigning them the tax income from a certain area instead of paying them in cash. In medieval Iran, this practice was designated by the Arabic

word *iqtâ* ("separation") and became a typical economic
institution that was, depending on the period and geographical region, implemented in different ways and sometimes
known by other names. However, the Saljuqs' army—which
as a standing army was typically composed of military
slaves of Turkish and, later on, Kurdish descent, among others—was considerably larger than that of the Buyids, if only
because the geographical extent of their empire was far
greater. For that reason the system of grants made to military leaders had to be systematically expanded and extended to areas in which it had earlier been practiced little or not
at all. Increasingly, grants were accompanied by additional
authority for the holder. Frequently the latter was given full
administrative powers and could appoint his own officials in
his grant. This broadened form of *iktâ*, which scholars usually call "administrative grants," became common everywhere under the Saljuqs, and was ultimately awarded even to
meritorious officials and court dignitaries. In times when
there was a strong central power, the system certainly had
advantages, and often had a stabilizing effect on internal
conditions. On the other hand, in this way more and more
local and regional centers of powers with their own troops
came into being. As a consequence of the increasing decline
of the Saljuq central government in the twelfth century and
the emergence of Atabeg dynasties, the grants, which had
originally been granted for a limited period of time, became
de facto and then also de jure hereditary, remaining in the
permanent possession of the military leaders and provincial
governors. In the later Saljuq period the granting of *iktâ* by
the state often amounted to no more than the legalization of

an already existing situation. After a few decades' interruption caused by the Mongol invasion in the thirteenth century, this tendency resumed in the fourteenth century.

Like other areas controlled by the Saljuqs, until the end of Malik-Shah's rule Iran's cities enjoyed widespread internal peace. Many of them profited from their position on the great trade routes, as did, for example, Kirman and Nishapur on the important route from the Persian Gulf to Khurasan. During the whole of the Saljuq period this latter route was a very important link between the Indian Ocean and the Arabian peninsula and Central Asia. Mediated by the Crusader states on the Syrian-Palestinian coast, the widespread trade network reached as far as Europe.

The Saljuq rulers admired Iranian culture, which they generously promoted. In their era, architecture and craftwork, for which the rulers presumably employed almost exclusively native Iranians, flourished. The Saljuqs, whose court language was Persian, also were active as patrons of Persian literature. Panegyric court poetry achieved perfection in the work of Anvari (d. c. 1170), who lived at Sanjar's court, and that of Khaqani (d. c. 1199), who wrote at various courts between Khwarezm and Shirvan; the great ruins of ancient Ctesiphon (al-Mada'in), whose vanished splendor seemed to him an admonition regarding the transience of all human striving, inspired Khaqanii to write one of the most famous poems in Persian literature. Nizami (1141-1209), who lived in Ganja, in Azerbaijan, under the rule of the Atabeg dynasty of the Eldeguzids, is considered the greatest representative of the romantic verse epic. His famous *Five Epics* (Arabic *khamseh*, "five," and Persian *panj ganj*, "five treasures"), which emphasize the ethical principle of humanity and are committed to the ideal image of the just ruler, became the classical model for later generations of Persian poets and for Turkish and Indian authors as well. Attar (d. between 1220 and 1234), who was from Nishapur and was one of Iran's greatest mystical storytellers, wrote in the eastern part of the Saljuq Empire; Jalal al-din al-Rumi (1207-1273, generally known in Iran as Mawlana) wrote in Anatolia (Rum) under the rule of the Anatolian branch of the Rum Saljuqs (1081-1307); his mystical epic was praised as the "Qur'an in Persian language." Here we must not forget to mention Omar Khayyam ("the tent-maker," died c. 1122), among the greatest figures of the Saljuq age. In Iran he famous chiefly as a brilliant mathematician and natural scientist, but in the West he is best known for his skeptical, ironic-satirical verse quatrains.

Sunnism and Shi'ism under the Saljuqs

The age of the Saljuqs was a time of intense religious unrest. At this point Shi'ism had split into two different factions: alongside "Twelver Shi'sm" and the moderate Zaydiyyah emerged the extremist Isma'iliyyah, which was itself divided into various smaller sects. The Isma'iliyah takes its name from Isma'il, the son of the sixth Shi'ite imam Ja'far. Although Isma'il predeceased his father, all the Isma'ilite groups recognize him as a true imam, whereas the Twelvers continue the succession of imams after Ja'far through the latter's younger son Musa (d. 799). The Isma'ilites developed an esoteric doctrine that included Gnostic and later also neo-Platonic elements. They assumed that there was a cyclic revelation that took place through six prophetic eras. Isma'il's hidden son Muhammad—who bore the same name as the Prophet—is expected to return as the *mahdi*. According to Isma'ilite doctrine, the mahdi will then do away with all religious systems, including Islam, and re-establish the paradisiacal, original religion of Adam; the latter has no fixed forms of worship and consists solely in God's creatures' praise of their Lord and in their recognition that he is the one and only God. Certain Isma'ili sects developed different conceptions of the mahdi, and some even proclaimed their leaders to be divine. In so doing, they clearly went beyond the limits set by orthodox Islam, which as a strict monotheistic religion does not allow any divine persons or beings other than God. Therefore many of the Ismailis' contemporaries no longer considered them Muslims at all.

By 900, the Isma'ilis had already created, by means of trained propagandists, a far-flung network that covered the whole Islamic world. Soon thereafter they gained political power and established an Isma'ilite counter-caliphate, that of the Fatimids (909-1171) in North Africa, and from the middle of the tenth century, in Egypt and Syria as well. The Isma'ilites' political goal was to overthrow the 'Abbasid caliphate and, from 1055 on, the battle against the Sunni Saljuq sultans and their followers.

In Iran, the Isma'ilite propaganda campaign was led by Hasan-i Sabbah (d. 1124) from Qum, who had originally been a Twelver Shi'ite but converted to the Isma'iliyah while he was young, and who had since 1072 been active as a propagandist in various parts of the country. In 1090 he conquered the fortress of Alamut in the eastern Alburz Mountains, where he henceforth resided. From there, he sent out envoys who were to incite open insurrection against the caliphs and the Saljuq rulers. The numerous political assassinations carried out by Hasan-i Sabbah's followers to weaken the Saljuq Empire became notorious. In Syria, they were given the Arabic name *hashishiyya*, "hashish-eaters," from which the Western term "Assassins" is derived, although their use of hashish and other drugs has not been proven. The "Assassins" referred to themselves as "devotees" (Persian *fida'in*, "those who sacrifice themselves"), since their activities usually cost them their lives. During Hasan-i Sabbah's lifetime, they thoroughly infiltrated the Saljuq army and court. One of the Assassins' most prominent victims was the vizier Nizam al-Mulk, who was stabbed by a disguised attacker in 1092. After Hasan-i Sabbah's death a dynasty of propagandists ruled in Alamut. They assassinated two caliphs, a Saljuq sultan, several governors and viziers, and numerous jurists who had preached or written against the Assassins. In 1256 the Mongols put an end to the rule of this sect, wrecked Alamut and other fortresses held by the Assassins, and destroyed the Isma'ilite library at Alamut. As late as the sixteenth century there were still Isma'ilite groups in the region, and today small Isma'ilite communities persist in Khurasan, Kirman, Yazd, and elsewhere.

The Saljuqs did all they could to establish orthodox Sunnism in their empire. To this end they promoted Sunni schools and teachers of the recognized Sunni schools of law. Theological seminaries or madrasahs (Arabic *madrasah*, lit., "place of teaching and learning") were set up throughout the empire, and thus education, which had previously been dispensed for the most part privately in mosques, was institutionalized. While the sultans had already distinguished themselves as founders of madrasahs, the latter are associated above all with the vizier Nizam al-Mulk. He established numerous madrasahs, named "Nizamiyyah" in honor of him, and staffed them with the most learned men of his time. The most famous Nizamiyah was in Baghdad; others were in Basra, Mosul, Isfahan, Nishapur, Herat, Marv, and Balkh.

Although the relationship between Sunnis and Shi'ites was seldom without tension, in general the non-Isma'ilite Shi'ites, a religious minority, seem to have lived quite peacefully alongside the Sunnis. Their common opponent, the Isma'ilites, seems to have ensured a relatively calm relations between the two sects. After an initial decline at the beginning of the Saljuq period, the importance of Twelver Shi'ism gradually increased again. Many Twelvers rose to high administrative posts and even became viziers. These officials were inclined to provide money for the tombs of the imams and to build mausoleums for the imams' descendants (Persian *imamzadeh*). Twelver dignitaries created their own Shi'ite educational institutions on the model of the Sunni madrasahs, and financed them—as did the Sunnis—by means of revenues provided by religious donations.

The Mongol Invasion and Its Consequences

The Mongol invasions under Genghis Khan (d. 1227) and his successors constituted a deep rupture in Iranian history. While it is true that there had already been a decline of cul-

tivated land and an increase of nomadism in Iran since the
Saljuq invasion in the eleventh century, the Mongol invasion
greatly accelerated this process, and this fact clearly distinguishes Mongol rule over Iran from the conquests and
dynastic shifts of the preceding centuries. The Mongol
homeland lay in the steppes of Central Asia, near the head-
waters of the great Siberian rivers west and northwest of
China, where they were nomadic shepherds and horsemen
divided, like the Turkish peoples, into tribes living in the
same region. Through a series of battles the Mongol prince
Timujin succeeded in uniting all the warring Mongol tribes
under his leadership. In 1206 he was formally recognized as
the master of all Mongols, and assumed the title Genghis
Khan. The meaning of this title is not clear; a connection
with the Turkish *tengiz*, "ocean," has often been suggested,
so that the title might be rendered as "universal ruler." After
conquering Transoxania and Khwarezm in the fall of 1219,
the Mongols invaded Iran, penetrating as far as the Caucasus. However, when in 1224 Genghis Khan moved back
toward the east, with the exception of Khurasan the country was once again left to itself until Genghis Khan's grandson Hülegü renewed the campaign of conquest in the West
and founded the Mongol Il-Khanid Empire.

The Mongol invasion was for Iran a catastrophe of unprecedented magnitude. The regions conquered by the Mongols
were left completely in ruins. Many areas recovered only
slowly, others not at all. The merciless cruelty with which the
Mongols carried out their campaigns, the countless mas-
sacres of the male population of the cities they conquered
and their enslavement of women and children severely dam-

aged the country. Political and intellectual centers of the Iranian cultural sphere such as Nishapur, Balkh, and Marv never regained their earlier significance as foci of Islamic civilization. Numerous other cities dwindled into villages. During their campaigns of conquest in Iran the Mongols spared only those craftsmen, artists, scholars, and families of notables in the cities who could be of use to them because of their experience in administration and jurisprudence. In this way the Iranian upper class remained, at least in the cities, relatively stable.

The conflicts between Iranians and Turks that arose during the Saljuq period were intensified by Mongol rule because many Turkish warriors followed Genghis Khan's army from Central Asia. It is generally thought that far more Turks than Mongols reached Iran. In the course of time the Mongols as a race were completely absorbed by the Turks. Hence in the long run Iran was not so much Mongolized as Turkified. After the Mongol invasion, the twofold ethnic nature of the population and thus of the society became a permanent feature of Iran. Even in today's Iran, Turks constitute independent population groups in northwest Iran, on the southern coast of the Caspian Sea, and in Khurasan.

The Mongols left neither longstanding ethnic nor linguistic traces on Iran. In particular, the Turkish language gained importance at the expense of Mongolian, but far more at that of Persian. Many areas of Iran became primarily Turkish-speaking and have remained so down to the present day. In the thirteenth century northwest Iran in particular became an area settled almost exclusively by Turks. Azari,

the language of Azerbaijan, was originally the name for the
Persian dialect spoken in that area; it was later transferred to
Turkish, which is still called Azeri there.

The Il-Khans

Genghis Khan decreed that after his death the vast empire
he had conquered should be divided among his four sons by
his first wife. At the beginning, the empire was still headed
by a Great Khan elected by a general assembly of Mongol
notables. His seat was Karakorum on the upper reaches of
the Orchon River in modern-day Mongolia. But in the
course of the following decades the ties holding together the
Great Khan's far-flung empire had grown so loose that by
the end of the thirteenth century independent Mongol states
had sprung up. From Iran, Mesopotamia, the Caucasus, and
Anatolia emerged the Il-Khanid Empire (1256-1335). Its
true founder was Hülegü (reigned 1256-1265), a grandson of
Genghis Khan who had continued the Mongol campaign of
conquest in West Asia. He began his campaigns in the spring
of 1253; in 1258 he took Baghdad and overthrew the 'Abbasid caliphate, which was thus extinguished after a rule of
more than five hundred years and found only an insignificant epilogue in the Egypt of the Mamluks (1250-1517). It
was also the Mamluks who in 1260 defeated Hülegü's troops
in Palestine and put a definitive end to his conquests in the
West. As nomadic shepherds and horsemen, the Mongols
settled—like the Turkish tribes that had immigrated from
Central Asia—particularly in areas that offered suitable climatic conditions for their flocks: in northwest Iran, in the

area around Baghdad, and in eastern Anatolia. It was here that the centers of Il-Khanid rule developed. The title "Il-Khan" which means something like "subordinate Khan," was assumed by Hülegü and his successors in deference to the Great Khan in Karakorum. Only toward the end of the thirteenth century did the Il-Khanid Empire finally detach itself from its subordination to the Great Khan. The Il-Khan Ghazan (ruled 1295-1304) formally cut his ties to the Great Khan and abandoned the title "Il-Khan" in favor of "Khan" on his coins and in his documents.

The Il-Khans succeeded in defending their empire against pressure exerted by neighboring states: in the east, against the Mongol autonomous region Chagatai, where the Amu Darya river (the ancient Oxus) became a permanent barrier; in the Caucasus, against the Golden Horde—also an autonomous Mongol state; in Egypt and in Syria, where the Euphrates formed the border, against the Mamluk state. Thus the Il-Khans ruled approximately the area that corresponded to Persia in both earlier and later times. The Il-Khanid Empire was essentially an Iranian state, whereas the center of Arab-Islamic culture shifted definitively to the west, away from conquered Mesopotamia and toward Cairo and Damascus. The increased division between the Arab and Iranian parts of the Islamic world ensuing from this situation becaem even deeper in later times, because the Mongol and Turkish rulers of Iran, Asia Minor, Central Asia, and India increasingly integrated themselves into the Iranian world with respect to language, government, and cultural orientation.

At the head of the state stood the Il-Khan, along with the

imperial assembly of Mongol nobles and high dignitaries, and especially the vizier, who was usually of Iranian descent. Il-Khan rulers did not, however, govern the state in accord with any firmly established forms. For example, over long periods of time there was not a single vizier, but rather two viziers holding office at the same time, and their rivalries made consistent exercise of the office impossible. Throughout the rule of the Il-Khans, the highest levels of government remained erratic, and this contributed to the relatively short duration of their empire. To this also contributed the numerous economic ills that became habitual under the Il-Khans. The henceforth constantly high level of nomads among the population was accompanied by systematic transformations of large areas of farmland into the pastures needed by the nomads for their herds. Together with the devastation that resulted from the Mongol invasions, this practice eventually led to a dramatic decrease in agricultural production. Because of these changes, the situation of the sedentary population grew more difficult, especially because the Mongol rulers and their followers were not competent in financial management. External wars and internal power struggles, extravagant expenditures at the imperial court, excessive distributions of money on the occasion of important events, and not infrequent successions to the throne— all this led inevitably to the financial draining and impoverishment of the sedentary population and in the long run undermined the country's fiscal resources.

In Iran, Mongol rule left a permanent mark on the system of government. The taxes arbitrarily introduced by the Il-Khans (e.g., on cattle and various commercial articles) were never rescinded; despite the fact that they were unsanctioned by Islamic law, they were preserved very officially. In later times no serious effort was made to bring these un-Islamic administrative factors into compliance with Islamic religious law. From the time of the Mongols, there was a de facto separation between government and Islamic law, and this situation was ultimately—after initial but increasingly muffled criticism from learned circles—tolerated by Muslim theologians as well.

The end of the Il-Khanid Empire came in 1335 with the assassination of the Il-Khan Abu Saʿid; he was the last Mongol ruler whose power still extended over the whole empire. After his death the country was fought over by warring emirs, tribes, and clans that sought to raise to power princes descended from Genghis Khan who were likely to benefit them; but in this they failed. Around the middle of the fourteenth century Mongol rule over Iran came to a definitive end, and the country disintegrated once again into various small regional states.

In this time of turmoil there lived in Fars—where the Atabeg dynasty of the Salghurids held power until 1282— one of the greatest poets of Iran, Saʿdi (1213/1219-1292), who had settled in his home town of Shiraz after years of journeying. His *Gulistan* ("Rose Garden") is a masterpiece of Persian prose with intercalated verses that conveys general wisdom about life in the form of ethical and didactic stories and anecdotes. Saʿdi's poetry is also highly regarded, especially his ghazals. In the twelfth century the *ghazal*, a short lyric form with erotic-mystical content, became a favorite poetic genre with erotic-mystical content. The main figure in the ghazal, the poet's handsome young male friend and lover, was often transformed by the poets into an abstract symbol in which they celebrated the appearance of divine beauty in this world. Hafiz (c. 1325/1326-1389)—who also came from Shiraz, which was then ruled by the Musafirids (1334-1393), a successor dynasty of the Il-Khans —is considered Iran's greatest ghazal poet; Goethe described him as his twin brother. With incomparable mastery Hafez makes the earthly and sensible converge with the divine and supersensible, keeping them both in play, and repeatedly completely transcends any univocal meaning.

Concepts of Rulership and Empire

By conquering Baghdad, Hülegü destroyed not only the center of the Islamic world, but also posed a serious challenge to the Muslim community's self-conception, because through this event Islam at first ceased to be a principle of political authority. Alongside legitimation based on Islam, after the Mongol invasion other views emerged that were based on nomadic traditions. For the next century and a half, Genghis Khan, the founder of an empire, became the quintessential model of the nomadic ruler. He was characterized by his mobility. His true residence was not a city, but rather the *ordu*, a mobile royal court-camp with no fixed location that accompanied him on his travels around his territory. The *ordu* was located outside fortified sites or cities and consisted of an extensive tent that could be expanded at any time. In the *ordu*, important political and military decisions were made, celebrations and entertainments held, ambassadors received, and, when necessary, documents prepared. The *ordu* usually included the ruler's family and entourage, military and civilian dignitaries, along with numerous servants, administrative employees, and poets and chroniclers who entertained the ruler with their art and recorded his deeds in writing. The notion that a ruler descended from nomads should have no fixed capital city was traced in later tradition back to Genghis Khan, although no categorical assertion to that effect has come down from him. While Mongols and Turks made certain centers into their capital cities and equipped them with splendid edifices, these could hardly be considered residences in the true sense, and they did not play a major role in the political and military domains. Instead, the capital city represented primarily a forum for scholarly and artistic activities that could not be pursued in the *ordu*, such as astronomy, architecture, and plastic arts. The *ordu* thus became a characteristic institution in the eastern Islamic lands between the thirteenth and the sixteenth centuries, even if in later times individual rulers sometimes also lived in the city and no longer exclusively in the *ordu*.

The Il-Khans called their empire "Iran." The idea of "Iran" as not only a purely geographical concept but also as a political concept, as it was defined in the age of the Sasanians (224-651), had by this time no longer existed for six centuries, as a result of the changed power relationships under the caliphate. Muslim geographers and chroniclers, even those who had been born in Iran, knew "Iran" only as a historical term designating the long-past Sasanian Empire. It is one of the notable facts of history that after all these centuries the name "Iran" came into use again as a political concept and an idea of empire under the Mongol Il-Khans, i.e., under non-Iranian sovereigns, and already occurs in the early chronicles of the age. This is also connected above all with the fact that with the end of the Baghdad caliphate, the Islamic universal empire also collapsed, so that other notions of rule could come into effect. In the extensive historical writing in Persian that was produced during the Il-Khanid age—during the Saljuq period, for the most part only works originally written in Arabic were translated into Persian—chroniclers saw in retrospect the centuries of the caliphate as a kind of interregnum, the rule of "regional princes," so to speak, between the Sasanian Empire and that of the Il-Khans, who had brought the individual provinces of Persia together into a unified empire again. That this occurred under non-Iranian rulers seems to have posed no problem for the chroniclers; perhaps the factual power of the Il-Khanid Empire reminded them of the old Iranian concept of empire known from Ferdowsi's *Shahnameh*. The city of Tabriz, the Mongols' most important city of residence, was apparently indivisibly associated with "Iran" as a political conception. The idea developed that Tabriz was—also after the Il-Khans—the "natural" capital of Iran. This idea lived on after 1600, when other cities—such as Isfahan and later Tehran—had assumed the role of capital. Tabriz continued to bear, as henceforth the second most important city in Iran, its official title of "Ruling City" (*dar al-saltaneh*, lit. "house of power"), which went back to the age of the Il-Khans, and in addition it was the usual residence of Persian crown princes and heirs to the throne.

Islam under Mongol Rule

The Il-Khans, their wives, and their entourage belonged to different religions, Buddhism in its Tibetan-Lamaist form and various kinds of Christianity being at first by far the most dominant. Until the end of the thirteenth century, the Il-Khans encouraged one or another of these religions, but never attempted to force their subjects to adopt a specific faith, because Genghis Khan was said to have ordered that all religions be tolerated in his empire. The Il-Khan Ghazan was the first to convert, in the initial year of his reign, 1295, to Sunni Islam. Ghazan's conversion, which made Islam the dominant religion once again, resulted in a far-reaching elimination of religious differences between the Mongols and their Iranian subjects, on the one hand, and on the other between the Mongols and the Turks living in the country, most of whom were also Muslims.

From the thirteenth century on, a popular form of religiousness emerged that was characterized by certain phenomena that may have existed earlier as well, but whose frequency under the disastrous conditions of life in the Mongol period was nonetheless unprecedented. These included religious views and practices that deviated from orthodox Islam or that were compatible with it only with restrictions, such as belief in miracles, the veneration of saints, tomb worship, pilgrimages to non-canonical religious sites—in short, a mystically-colored religiousness that was chiefly a matter of invididual feeling and had little to do with orthodox theology; in Western scholarship, it is often termed "popular Islam." However, it was not connected solely with the com-

mon people; quite a few members of the wealthy and educated classes, military and civilian dignitaries, and even the
rulers themselves often turned to this kind of religiousness.

Islamic mysticism sees its goal above all in the personal,
individual experience of God. The mystics spoke of a "mystical path" on which the believer was driven forward by his
love of God and at whose end stood a vision of the Divine
or even a fusion of the soul with God in a state of supreme
ecstasy. By means of a gradual overcoming of the ego and
the rationality that they considered an impediment to the
experience of the Divine, the mystics sought to eliminate
this-worldly impressions from their consciousness and to
achieve a state of inner purification in which it would be
possible for human beings to become one with God. The
practices developed with this goal in mind include especially the repetition of a certain religious formula that can be
recited individually and silently or aloud in the community,
and also ecstatic dancing. The mystics were called "Sufis"
because of the woolen robe (from Arabic *suf*, "wool") they
wore, or "dervishes" (from Persian *darvish*, "poor"). Whereas originally these seekers after God generally gathered
around a mystical master who provided spiritual guidance
for them, in the time of the Mongols this personal master-
pupil relationship was already largely institutionalized, and
the previously small, mystical groups became communities
living in their own convents under definite, if still not very
rigid, rules. In the thirteenth and fourteenth centuries the
dervish communities increasingly lost their earlier esoteric
character. The dervishes and their leader, the sheikh (Arabic
shaykh, "venerable elder, master") were more and more seen

as the true representatives of Islamic religious belief. Their convents and tombs were places of popular worship. People ascribed miraculous powers to many dervishes and sought their help against repression and financial exploitation by officials.

Under the repressive living conditions connected with Mongol rule, some dervish communities developed into genuine mass movements. The common people came to them in droves because they hoped that a miracle-working sheikh could provide them with protection and help in everyday life. In fact, quite a few sheikhs saw themselves as advocates for the Iranian people in opposition to the rulers, and when conflicts arose they acted—sometimes successfully—as mediators between the two parties. On the basis of their growing economic prosperity resulting from the donations, endowments, and privileges they received from their followers, in the fourteenth century many dervish groups became well-organized, militant associations whose explosive political power repeatedly manifested itself, initially in a local and later in a wider, super-regional framework. Exemplary in this regard is the dervish community of the Safaviyyah, from which the Safavid dynasty (1501-1722) emerged.

Certain features of popular Islamic religiousness, such as a particularly intense reverence for ʿAli, show Shiʿite influences. However, it would be an error to deduce from this a formal conversion to Shiʿism, since popular Islam is characterized precisely by an oscillation between Sunnism and Shiʿism. On the other hand, it is understandable that the vast geographical spread of the mystical communities, from Anatolia to Central Asia, promoted veneration of ʿAli and his descendants and thus prepared the way for later Shiʿite propaganda. Thus, for example, Shiʿism could spread in Anatolia—a center for the Safavids—even though in that area there was as yet no Shiʿit literature.

Timur and His Successors

Timur (1336-1405), called "the lame" because of an injury he had received in his youth—hence the European corruption of his name from the Turkic Timur Lenk, "Timur the lame," to Tamerlane—came from the nomadic tribe of Barlas, which was probably Turkish, in Transoxania. After Genghis Khan, he was the greatest nomad ruler and founder of a major empire, and he caused further significant changes in the Iranian cultural sphere. The old Iranian area of Transoxania had been particularly severely affected by Mongol rule. Around 1370, Timur exploited the anarchical conditions there to make himself, as the young leader of a group of warlike adventurers who came chiefly from nomadic backgrounds, the supreme ruler of Transoxania. Ten years later he undertook the first campaign from Transoxania toward the west.

The model Timur sought throughout his life to emulate was Genghis Khan, whose empire he wanted to restore. Toward the end of his life he had almost achieved his goal: his empire reached from Transoxania to the Euphrates and the Caucasus. By conquering this enormous territory Timur, who was particularly drawn to Iranian culture, reunited for the last time the extensive ancient Iranian cultural sphere into a single empire. He died in 1405 during a campaign on the way to China. All in all, Timur's campaigns, which were as famous as they were feared among his contemporaries, were conducted with unbridled cruelty and even beastliness. As a symbol of this we can take the pyramids of skulls he caused to be piled up outside the gates of rebellious cities; these were the skulls not only of fallen opponents but also of the male and female inhabitants of the cities. Timur's reverence for his Mongol model Genghis Khan completely determined his image of himself. He never assumed the title of Khan; instead, throughout his life he ruled in the name of the puppet khans descended from Genghis Khan who were supposed to lend his rule a formal legitimation. He married a princess from Genghis Khan's family, so that he could claim affliation with his role-model. He called himself "amir" (Arabic, "commander"), and used the honorific *gurgen* (royal son-in-law), which identified him as related by marriage to Genghis Khan's descendants. In accord with nomadic tradition, he also clung to the *ordu* or mobile court-camp. Despite his firm connections with Mongol tradition, Timur often emphasized his Islamic belief; he was strongly influenced by the Sufi dervishes whom he kept in his entourage as spiritual advisors.

At the time of his death, Timur had established neither an arrangement for the appointment of the successor to his enormous territory nor even a stable institutional organization for it. Throughout his life he had sought to govern his empire through his personal authority and to ensure that he retained control over the conduct of state affairs. Therefore after his death the Timurid princes who had issued from his family were free to govern their various provinces with

almost complete independence. This quickly led to the fragmentation of the territory he had conquered. The Timurid
princes' neighbors took advantage of this situation: from the
west Turkmen tribal confederations advanced from eastern
Anatolia, first the Kara Koyunlu ("Black Sheep"), later the
Ak Koyunlu ("White Sheep")—so called, perhaps, because
of their totemic animals—, while the Turkish Uzbeks invaded Transoxania from the north and northeast. In 1507 the
rule of the Timurid rulers came to an end when the Uzbeks
conquered Khwarazm after taking Transoxania.

Thus the significance of the Timurid rulers hardly lies in
the area of military efficiency and statecraft. Above all, it
was their cultural and artistic achievements that made
Timur and his successors famous. In addition to Timur's
capital of Samarkand, which he ornamented—chiefly by
employing craftsmen and artists he had brought in from the
areas he had conquered—with splendid edifices built on
Persian models, in the second half of the fifteenth century
Herat emerged as another important Timurid cultural center. The rulers and their dignitaries were major patrons of
literature and poetry, miniature painting, the art of book-
binding, and calligraphy. Islamic Iran's greatest miniature
painter, Bihzad (d. 1535/1536) worked in Herat, as did the
dervish and poet Jami (1414-1492). The most important
achievement of the latter, who is considered the last classical
Iranian poet, were his epics, collected under the title *Haft
Owrang* ("The Seven Thrones" or "Ursa Major"). However,
in accordance with the still vital traditions of the steppes,
under Timur and his successors the *ordu* remained the political and military center of the empire. In order to combine

nomadic life in tents with the advantages and comforts of sedentary existence, the Timurids created exceptionally splendid gardens on the traditional Persian model, in which the *ordu* frequently resided. Around old cities such as Samarkand and Herat extensive garden areas were developed that differed from the suburbs of earlier times not only by their size, but also by the magnificent pavilions that were erected in them.

One of Timur's last descendants—and on his mother's side, a descendant of Genghis Khan himself—Zahir al-Din Babur, sought in vain to bring Transoxania back under Timurid control. After his final defeat, he moved into northern India, where he founded his own empire, that of the Mughals. There the flourishing culture of the Timurids, enriched by new elements, enjoyed a no less brilliant continuation.

The material basis for the Timurid state was also provided by the usual granting of fiscal grants in return for personal military assistance in the event of war. In the fourteenth century, the word *iqta* was increasingly replaced by the Mongol term *soyurghal* ("reward"); until the seventeenth century the term *tiyul* (also *toyul*, possibly an Iranized misspelling of the Turkish *yatul*, "landed property") was also used as a synonym of *soyurghal*. Typical phenomena of the fifteenth century were the grant-holder's independence in fiscal, administrative, and now even juridical matters, along with the inheritability of the grants and the considerable extent of the territories granted, which sometimes included whole provinces. Around this time the rural population had almost completely lost the right to own cultivated land; very few of the formerly free village communities still existed, and their further decline could not be prevented. The imperial administration under Timur's successors was the result of the now long-established ethnic dichotomy between Iranians and Turks. The supreme state authority (*divan*) was responsible, among other things, for maintaining the army, which consisted largely of Turks and Turkified Mongols. The civil and financial administration lay traditionally in the hands of native Iranians. This state of affairs was altered by neither the Mongols nor the Timurids, and thus a financial bureaucracy composed of Iranian officials working independently of the supreme *divan* continued to exist. The Mongol tradition also remained alive in fiscal institutions, and this meant above all that the Timurids also levied un-Islamic taxes, since the state was neither able nor willing to forego these lucrative sources of income.

Like the preceding centuries, that of the Timurids was essentially shaped by Islamic folk belief and its representatives, the popular mystical dervish communities. Because of the constant attraction the dervishes' religiousness had for the people and many rulers, the theological oppositions between Sunnis and Shiʿites became less manifest, so that it is often difficult to ascertain to which denomination a given individual or group belongs. Of course, orthodox Sunni theology continued to live on, but in the fifteenth century it had already largely fossilized into scholastic forms and limited itself—with a few exceptions—to composing countless glosses, commentaries, and commentaries on commentaries. Thus the representatives of Sunnism ultimately proved incapable of competing with the multiplicity of Shiʿite or heterodox movements. When one of these movements, the Safaviyyah, succeeded by force of arms in establishing itself and in making Twelver Shi'ism the state religion of Iran (1501), the fate of Sunnism in large areas of Timurid territory was sealed, though not in Transoxania, where the Uzbeks who invaded in the early sixteenth century were Sunnis.

CHAPTER III

Iran in the Early Modern Period (1501–1779)

A Qajar king during an audience with delegates from Europe

Turkish Immigration from the West

Toward the end of the fifteenth century the Islamic East was in a state of upheaval, after which new power blocs appeared: the Safavid Empire in Iran, with the Ottoman Empire on the west, and on the east the Uzbek Khanate in Transoxania and, about two decades later, the Indian Mughal Empire. Whereas since the eleventh century waves of Turkish immigration from Central Asia had essentially shaped Iran's history, at the beginning of the fifteenth century a reverse movement began to emerge that brought three great waves of Turkish nomads into Iran, this time coming from the west. The first two of these waves occurred under the Turkmen tribal confederations of the Kara Koyunlu and Ak Koyunlu, which came out of eastern Anatolia and overran large parts of the Timurid empire. Beginning in the age of the Saljuqs, Muslim chroniclers and geographers generally used the term "Turkmen"—which today generally designates the Turkish tribes that have spread since the Middle Ages over the Near and Middle East and Central Asia—to refer to the tribes of Oghuz origin that had converted to Islam. Since the Mongol periods, the term "Turkmen" had largely replaced the term "Oghuz." For nearly a century

(1380-1469) the Kara Koyunlu ruled in Iran and Azerbaijan, but they were then displaced by the Ak Koyunlu (1396-1508), who for a short time controlled the whole area from Anatolia to Khurasan and as far as the Persian Gulf, so that it seemed to many contemporaries that they were to be the future dominant power in the East.

The third wave of Turkish immigration from Anatolia to the Iranian plateau, which took on significant proportions, involved the Turkmen tribe of the Kizilbash (Turkish, "red heads"), fanatical adherents of the Safavids who at the beginning of the sixteenth century had broken the power of the Ak Koyunlu and seized power in Iran for themselves. The beginnings of the Safavid dynasty first become visible in northwest Iran in the time of the Il-Khans. The ancestor from whom they took their name, Safi al-Din (d. 1334), had around 1300 established an originally Sunni-oriented dervish convent, called Safaviyyah after him, in the city of Ardabil. We know very little about Safi al-Din's ancestors, except that he came from a well-to-do family of farmers and cattle-breeders that resided near Ardabil and presumably had Kurdish roots.

At the outset, the order of the Safaviyyah may not have differed from many other dervish communities, yet the political development to which it led was unique. Its founder Safi al-Din was a typical figure of folk Islam, venerated as a saint by his followers, who attributed various miracles to him.

As the leader of an order, Safi al-Din achieved considerable success and laid he foundation for his community's future prosperity. His no less gifted successors at the head of the order amassed immense wealth and systematically sought to organize their numerous followers into military units. For a long time the order attracted enormous numbers of recruits from Turkmen nomadic tribes in eastern Anatolia, Azerbaijan, and northern Syria—areas that belonged at least in part to the Ottoman Empire, but in which Safavid agents nevertheless openly carried on deliberate and successful propaganda efforts. Although they were nominally Muslims, the Turkmen tended to adopt extreme religious views, so that their Islamic creed is with some justification interpreted as only a superficially Islamized paganism in which the shamanistic traditions of their homeland on the steppes of Inner Asia can still be clearly discerned beneath a thin overlay of Islam. The long-standing, close connection between these nomads and Sufism, combined with their enthusiasm for religious war, led Turkmen to join the Safaviyyah in large numbers. A further factor was the policy pursued by the Ottomans, who had by this time expanded their territory far to the east and were now seeking to subject the Turkmen tribes of Anatolia to the rigid administrative structures of their empire. The Turkmen, whom the government had up to that point left largely undisturbed, rejected the Sultan's demand that they pay taxes and provide soldiers for the Ottoman army, and increasingly they shifted their political and religious allegiance to the leaders of the Safavid orders. Haydar (d. 1488), the head of one such order, wore, allegedly because of a dream in which ʿAli had appeared to him, a red cap with twelve pleats that has often been interpreted as a symbol of the twelve imams of Shiʿism. Because of the cap's color, its wearers were called Kizilbash ("red heads") by their opponents, but they themselves quickly adopted this name as an honorary title. Sometime around the middle of the fifteenth century the Safaviyyah order was transformed from a mystical popular movement into a tightly organized and well-armed community of Turkmen religious warriors.

For Iran, and especially for the Iranian plateau, the three waves of immigration by Turkish nomadic tribes meant a further increase in the number of nomads; the latter could not move on beyond Iran because since the sixteenth century the Uzbeks had constituted an unrelenting military barrier in the east. In this way Iran became for centuries afterward a permanent homeland for countless hordes of Turkish nomads, whom the emergence of the new power blocs prevented from spreading to new territories. The disputes over pastureland that inevitably resulted from this led many conflicts between tribes and tribal confederations. In the long run, did not induce the tribes to abandon their nomadic way of life but it did induce them to change the way they were organized: they transformed themselves from originally economically-determined communities into more or less military structures. Only the nomads' politico-military authority over the sedentary population that fed them permitted them to survive in their traditional way of life. It is no wonder that under these conditions the repression and exploitation of the Iranian people working the land once again greatly increased. The military supremacy of the nomadic tribes continued to be a factor in Iranian history over the following centuries as well. Only at the beginning of the twentieth century was the central government able gradually to supplant the tribes as the dominant military power.

The Safavids

The Safavid period (1501-1722) is another crucial turning point in Iran's history. Whereas since the Arab conquest in the seventh century Iran had been part of the great Islamic community that was disintegrating into regional powers after eight and a half centuries of foreign domination and political fragmentation, the Safavids reestablished a strong and enduring state on Iranian soil. This was the dynasty that introduced Twelver Shi'ism as the state religion of Iran and thereby brought the Shi'ah to power on its territory. Thus began the religious shaping of Iran—which was at that point still primarily Sunni—as a Shi'ite country, which it has remained down to the present day, even though this process went on at least until the end of the Safavid period. The conversion to Shi'ism is the element that most obviously distinguishes modern Iran from its neighbors. The process of transforming Iran into a homogeneous Twelver Shi'ite land, along with Iran's geopolitical situation between the Sunni blocs of the Ottoman Empire, the Uzbek Khanate, and the Indian Mughal Empire, over time contributed to the development among most of Iran's heterogeneous population of a new-found feeling of religious unity on the basis of Twelver Shi'ism. However, the unification of extensive Persian-speaking areas of the Islamic East under Safavid rule should not be interpreted, as it sometimes has been, as the beginning of a future Iranian nation-state or as a breakthrough of Iranian national consciousness. Until the twentieth century the self-conception of both Iranians and Turks living on Iranian soil was based on their common adherence to Shi'ism, which for them represented true Islam.

In 1501 Isma'il, the young head of the Safavid order, conquered the city of Tabriz with the help of the Kizilbash
tribes and resumed an ancient Iranian royal tradition by taking the title *shahanshah* ("king of kings"). During the following nine years he extended his control over all of Iran,
Mesopotamia, and western Afghanistan. This first Safavid
shah already entered into military conflicts with the
Ottomans in the west and the Uzbeks in the east that continued under the following Safavid rulers. In general, this
enmity is blamed on the religious opposition between Shi'ite
Iran and the Sunni Ottomans and Uzbeks, but at least as
great a role was played—regardless of religious propaganda
on both sides—by substantial political and territorial interests. The Safavids competed with the Uzbeks for possession
of the province of Khurasan, which they were eventually
able to secure for themselves. However, border cities such as
Herat and Mashhad repeatedly fell under the temporary
control of the Uzbeks. Well into the nineteenth century the
Turkmen carried out attacks over the border in search of
booty and slaves.

Conflict with the Ottoman Empire, which in the sixteenth
century was at the height of its power, was inevitable. The
Ottoman sultans sought to control the unrest among the
Kizilbash in eastern Anatolia, who were devoted to the
Safavids, in order to provoke a military decision. In the fall
of 1514 Sultan Selim I (reigned 1512-1520) soundly defeated the Safavid army at the battle of Chaldiran in eastern
Azerbaijan. The Ottoman victory was due above all to their
being equipped with modern artillery and firearms, which
the Iranian army still lacked. The new weapons had been

known in Iran for a long time, but in contrast to the Ottomans, the Iranians at first accepted them only with a certain hesitation. The Kizilbash voluntarily forewent firearms because this way of fighting seemed to them unmanly and cowardly; their persistence in fighting a moving battle on horseback led to their doom, because the Ottoman artillery did devastating damage to their cavalry. With the defeat at Chaldiran ended the previously successful expansion of the Safavid Empire; still more, it caused Shah Isma'il's aura of invincibility among his Kizilbash followers to evaporate. During the last decade of his reign he no longer engaged in any military campaigns. However, contrary to the earlier notion that at this point the shah entirely ceased any politico-military activity, Ottoman and Venetian sources show him to have been a clever organizer and far-sighted politician who undertook many and diverse diplomatic efforts to modernize his army's weaponry and— successfully—to protect the young Safavid state against further Ottoman attack and thus to ensure its survival.

Under Isma'il's successor Tahmasp (reigned 1524-1576), invasions by the Uzbeks and conflicts with the Ottomans continued; Mesopotamia was lost to the Ottoman Empire. Despite the continuing clashes between Safavids and Ottomans during the whole sixteenth century, attempts at diplomatic contact were repeatedly undertaken. The Safavids had a great interest in ensuring that Shi'ite pilgrims could safely visit the shrines of their imams in Iraq and the holy cities of Mecca and Medina; since the Hijaz had fallen to the Ottomans (1517), these places were also under Ottoman control.

The reign of Shah ʿAbbas I (1588-1629), commonly called "the Great," marks the highpoint of Safavid rule. Under his rule the empire reached its greatest extent; he centralized governmental administration, encouraged economic development, and promoted architecture and art. He was able to recover most the territory that had been lost under his predecessors as a result of internal conflicts: he took Khurasan back from the Uzbeks (1598/99), Azerbaijan (1603/04) and large parts of Iraq, including Baghdad and southeast Anatolia from the Ottomans (1623/24), and the area of Kandahar in western Afghanistan from the Mughal emperors (1622). After the shah's death, however, many of the territories he had subdued were once again lost to the Ottoman Empire. In 1639 the treaty of Zuhab (or Qasr-i Shirin) settled the boundaries between Safavid and Ottoman territory, and except for the northern section these boundaries have lasted down to the present day. For Iran, however, this treaty brought about the final loss of Iraq and the Shiʿite holy sites.

The successors of ʿAbbas I were for the most part incompetent rulers, with the sole exception of his namesake ʿAbbas II (ruled 1642-1666). Toward the end of the century, when the Safavid shahs' loss of power could no longer be ignored, internal economic problems and religiously motivated rebellions brought the empire into a crisis. In 1722, the Afghan Ghalzai tribe invaded Iran and conquered large areas of the country. The last Safavid shah, Sultan Husayn (ruled 1694-1722) was forced to abdicate in the fall of the same year.

During the Safavid period diplomatic and commercial contacts with Europe of an unprecedented extent were established. Europe's interest in Safavid Iran was directly connected with the threatening power of the Ottoman Empire, to which both parties were exposed. Religious considerations apparently played no role for either side. Despite numerous embassies, however, no tangible military result was achieved since the distance separating Europe from Iran, with its strains and dangers, proved too great an impediment. Toward the end of the sixteenth century the focus of European-Iranian contacts shifted increasingly from foreign policy toward trade and economic relations. In the wake with European diplomatic missions and trading came numerous researchers eager to learn about the country, and they left us an abundance of informative travel reports about Safavid Persia.

Again, it was chiefly Shah ʿAbbas I who took a great interest in promoting foreign trade and who sought to attract European merchants to the country. On the European side, since the sixteenth century foreign trade had increasingly been conducted by large state companies that had the advantage of a broad capital base. During the seventeenth century the British East India Company, founded in 1600, and the Dutch East India Company (*Oost Indische Compagnie*, founded in 1602) competed with each other for trade with Asia, and both were inerested in establishing commercial relationships with Iran. Commercial goods from Iran—chiefly silk, cloth, and spices—were transported over the traditional caravan routes by way of Baghdad and Aleppo to the Mediterranean or by way of Tabriz and Trebizond to the Black Sea. However, since both routes passed through Ottoman territory, they were burdened with transit tolls and were not usable in times of war. The sea route to Europe that the Portuguese under Vasco da Gama (1469-1524) had opened as early as 1497/98 by sailing around the Cape of Good Hope remained for the time being unavailable to Iran. The Portuguese had immediately recognized the strategic and commercially favorable situation of the island of Hormuz at the entrance to the Persian Gulf and took permanent control of it in 1515. During the sixteenth century the Portuguese held a virtual monopoly over sea trade on the Indian Ocean, which Shah ʿAbbas was first able to break in 1623 with the aid of a fleet provided by the British East India Company. After he had reconquered Hormuz and destroyed the island city, the settlement on the south coast of the mainland, where British, Dutch, and French agents had established themselves some time earlier in competition with Hormuz, was developed under the name of Bandar ʿAbbas (Persian *bandar*, "harbor") into a major trading post.

The destruction of the Portuguese commercial base in Hormuz opened the way for trade activities in the Persian Gulf on the part of the new sea powers Great Britain and Holland. On the Iranian side, Armenian merchants played an important role by establishing trade depots in Europe. In order to take advantage of the Armenians' commercial experience and craft abilities, Shah ʿAbbas had several thousand Armenian families from Azerbaijan transferred to his new residence of Isfahan (1604), where he assigned them their own quarter that bore the name of their old home city of Julfa and has remained the city's Armenian neighborhood down to the present day.

By the end of the seventeenth century the rivalry between the British and Dutch East India Companies for dominance in the Persian Gulf had been settled in favor of the former. However, the decline of the Safavid Empire was accompanied by a decline of security in the Gulf, which was increasingly plagued by pirates (mostly Arab, but also British). Nonetheless, the East India Company continued its trade activities in Bandar ʿAbbas and later in Basra, in southern Iraq, even though they were reduced in scope. During the eighteenth century trade relationships with Czarist Russia were intensified. After the eighteenth century, European interests in Iran, which had previously been oriented exclusively toward trade, turned into a power struggle among the great European nations for political influence in the Middle East.

The Safavid State

The Safavids claimed to be descended from the seventh imam, Musa al-Kazim ("the self-controlled," d. 799), in direct lineage from the Prophet Muhammad. This claim cannot be proven beyond doubt, but in any case the oldest extant sources for the early history of the Safavids explicitly state that they were members of ʿAli's family. This ancestry of the Safavids was nonetheless considered to be authentic, and it lent them great religious prestige that allowed them to present themselves as the sole representatives and deputies of the hidden twelfth imam. Thus the highest religious and worldly authorities were united in the person of the Safavid shah and formed the basis for a claim to universal power

such as had not been made since the fall of the ʿAbbasid
caliphate. At the same time, in this personal union the
Safavids were the leaders of the Safaviyyah order. However,
they were not able to integrate the Sufi organization of the
order into the state administration, so that as time went on
Sufism became increasingly insignificant. It can be said that
through Sufism the Kizilbash were affiliated in a special way
with the shah, but when Shah ʿAbbas succeeded in weakening the power of the tribes, Sufism lost all political influence.
The Safavids' legacy of the long Iranian royal tradition was
taken over by later dynasties, but they could not lay claim to
the religious aura that surrounded the Safavid shahs. Thus,
after the fall of the Safavid Empire in 1722, numerous
princes who were genuinely or allegedly descended from the
Safavid family arose throughout the land as pretenders to
the throne and were used by the new holders of power to
legitimate their own rule.

During the sixteenth century the Kizilbash tribes, with
whose help the Safavids had come to power, were able to
assert their predominant position in the government.
Turkmen were appointed to military offices and provincial
governorships, and the Kizilbash leaders to whom a
province was given to administer generally took their tribes-
men with them, thus preserving the tribe's unity. Consequently, the Safavid Empire was at first in no way a centralized state, but instead was based on the rule of nomadic
tribes; to this corresponded the Safavid shahs' continuing
use of the *ordu*. Militarily, the Safavids long remained completely dependent on the Kizilbash. In addition, the shahs
followed the usual practice of rewarding Kizilbash leaders

for their military service by fiscal grants. As under earlier dynasties, under the Safavids these grants were de facto inheritable and the property of the military leader. From the outset, the Safavids tried to control the latent instability of the empire, which was in constant danger of disintegrating into independent areas under the rule of Kizilbash tribes, by filling posts in the civil administration with Iranian officials, whereas military posts went largely to the Kizilbash. Because of their experience and sedentary way of life these Iranian officials represented a more reliable foundation for the State than did the Kizilbash.

Shah ʿAbbas I was the first to succeed in centralizing the state administrative apparatus and eliminating the predominant position of the Kizilbash. Under his government began the steady decline of the Turkmen tribes and the decay of their military influence. Soon after he mounted the throne, ʿAbbas created—largely following the model of the janissaries in the Ottoman Empire—a standing army with cavalry, infantry, and artillery units. He admitted two British adventurers, the brothers Robert and Anthony Sherley, to his court in order to take advantage of their knowledge of the techniques of artillery. However, the notion that the Sherleys actually introduced artillery in Iran is erroneous, because it was already known there in Ismaʿil's time. The shah's new army was composed of the so-called "king's servants" (Persian *ghulaman*, Turkish *kullar*, "military slaves"), for the most part Caucasian Christians (Georgians, Armenians, etc.) who had been taken prisoner during the Safavids' campaigns, converted to Islam, and trained for service at the court. These military slaves were no longer loyal to a particular tribe but exclusively to the shah, who found in them valuable support against the Kizilbash. Caucasians were appointed to newly created military posts such as the supreme commander of the king's servants and the riflemen, and ultimately also to the new posts of supreme commander of all the Safavid military forces (Persian *sardar-i lashkar*). Thereby the inevitable disputes between Turkmen and Iranians regarding these high posts were effectively forestalled, because depriving the Kizilbash of power had inevitably increased the influence of the Iranian civil officials, and especially that of the vizier. Filling the new posts with king's servants, who by the beginning of the seventeenth century held about a fifth of all the high state offices, ensured the cohesion of the army. In addition, Shah ʿAbbas systematically resettled Kizilbash groups and scattered them over Iranian territory in order to weaken their tribal ties.

Although Shah ʿAbbas managed to establish a balance between the three groups that provided the basis for the state—the Turkmen, the Iranians, and the Caucasians—the measures he took proved to be only temporarily successful and in the long run contributed to the decline of the Safavids. The new royal troops were paid—unlike the Kizilbash —from the revenues of the estates under the crown's direct control. At the expense of the Kizilbash, large tracts of land in the provinces were now added to the royal domains, and members of the king's servants were appointed to manage them and to collect taxes for the state coffers. However, in the long run the decrease in the number of Kizilbash governors was accompanied by increased financial exploitation of the royal domains, since the king's servants did not live from the land itself as did the Kizilbash but rather, during their tenure of office, tried to squeeze as much as possible out of the lands under their control. Excessive taxation (which impoverished the rural population and consequently increased the already considerable burden of taxes) imposed to meet the demands of the court and the military was one of the main causes for the decline of the state.

A further factor was the incompetence of Shah ʿAbbas's successors. This can also be traced back to a fateful step taken earlier, because for fear of conspiracies ʿAbbas had abandoned the previous custom of sending young princes to the provinces, where they were supposed to gain practical experience in administration under the guidance of Kizilbash leaders. Instead, ʿAbbas shut up his own sons in the harem, where they were exposed to the influence of the women and eunuchs at the court and could acquire no experience of government. When later on they themselves came to power, they often showed little inclination to devote themselves to affairs of state. The shahs who succeeded ʿAbbas continued to raise the princes in the harem; intrigues woven by military officials, court officers, eunuchs, princesses, and concubines were the result. Increasing economic problems as well as religious unrest and rebellions, provoked especially by the last Safavid Sultan Husayn's ill-fated persecution of the Sunnis living in Iran, contributed to the further destabilization of the empire, whose end—despite an epilogue played out during the short reign of various Safavid puppet rulers—was finally sealed with the abdication of Sultan Hoseyn in 1722.

The cultural legacy of the age of the Safavids is insepara-

ble from the city of Isfahan, which Shah ʿAbbas I chose as
his capital around 1600 and developed into a splendid residence that can still rightly claim to have some of the most
beautiful architectural monuments in the world. To the
south and southwest of the old city center with its winding
streets, which dates primarily from the age of the Saljuqs,
the shah built his splendid new residence area with inge-
niously planned avenues and extensive gardens. At its center
is the enormous royal square, which at that time, according
to reports by European travelers, surpassed anything in the
Western world. In Isfahan, Iran's artistic creation reached
another highpoint: Shah ʿAbbas called upon craftsmen,
architects, and artists from all over the country to produce
the city's many incomparable edifices covered with bands of
decorative script and complicated patterns of glazed faience.
Under Shah ʿAbbas Isfahan became a cosmopolitan city
that is said to have rapidly grown from an original population of about 60,000 inhabitants to ten times that number.
Many European contemporaries provided a colorful picture
of the city: they described a lively mixture of Iranians,
Turks, Europeans, Chinese, and Indians; Muslims, Zoroastrians, Christians, Jews, and Hindus.

Shiʿism under the Safavids

Immediately after taking Tabriz, the young Shah Ismaʿil
declared Twelver Shiʿism to be the state religion. What led
him to do so has still not been fully explained. It is certain
that along with its growing militancy the Safaviyyah order
had also undergone a fundamental religious transformation.

Although this process of transformation is not clear in every detail, it is noteworthy that none of the main chroniclers of the time, not even those who opposed the Safavids, described any of Ismaʿil's ancestors as a Shiʿite. The Turkmen's idolization of their Safavid leaders, which was noted by contemporaries and which spurred them to an almost unbridled willingness to sacrifice themselves on the battlefield, profoundly influenced Ismaʿil himself. The *Divan* (collection of poems) in Turkish, the language of the Kizilbash, that Ismaʿil composed in his youth and which is programmatic in nature, reveals a very personal, extremely religious sense of mission that has nothing to do with orthodox Twelver Shiʿism and everything to do with the views of the Kizilbash tribes: in his poems Ismaʿil describes himself as an incarnation of divine substance and even as the returned twelfth imam, the mahdi. Although this extreme conception did not prevail in the long run, it nonetheless remains a remarkable fact that the introduction of Twelver Shiʿism as the state religion was initiated by a man whose understanding of the elaborate Twelver theology was hazy at best. In any case, with Ismaʿil begins a new polarization between Sunni and Shiʿite Islam. His strong, indeed aggressive anti-Sunni animosity culminated in his demand that all his subjects publicly curse the first three caliphs as an outward sign of their Shiʿite attitude. Here began an ideologization of Shiʿite religion that created a deep gulf between Sunnis and Shiʿites and reawakened acute oppositions that had become less sharp by the fifteenth century.

The Twelver Shiʿite state religion imposed from above was at first accepted by the still mainly Sunni population of Iran with the greatest reluctance and could be spread only by means of coercive measures. Many scholars who refused to adopt the new religious direction lost their lives or fled to the neighboring Sunni states. At the beginning of the sixteenth century, there was as yet no Twelver Shiʿite tradition in Iran. Thus it is questionable whether Ismaʿil and his followers could have succeeded in forcing a whole people to adopt a new faith without the support of Arab Shiʿite scholars from Bahrain, southern Lebanon, and southern Iraq— traditional Shiʿite centers—who were brought into the country to explain the doctrine of Twelver Shiʿism and make it accessible to the population. It was because of their work that Shiʿism finally abandoned its extreme elements and its popular form. These scholars developed the learned structure of Twelver orthodoxy into the form it has kept down to the present day, so that the religious orientation of the Safavid Empire became increasingly distant from its popular origin as represented by the Kizilbash, and thereby from Sufism as well. In the course of the seventeenth century, the term "Sufi," which was once an honorable name for the Safavids' followers, came to mean "heretic."

Under the rule of the Safavids, for the first time in the history of Twelver Shiʿism scholars were able to form independent social groups without being repressed by the state. The Shiʿite clergy first achieved its final form in the eighteenth century, but in the age of the Safavids the foundations were already laid for the development of a status that can properly be called "clerical"; however, unlike in Christianity, "clerics" are not ordained priests, but rather simply scholars (Arabic *ulama*) who have completed studies of the religious and legal traditions of Shi'ism. The Persian title of these scholars, which is also used in a very similar way by Sunni Islam, is "mullah" (from Arabic *mawla*, "master") or "akhund" (Persian, "teacher").

The hierarchical organization of the Shi'ite clergy began under Shah Isma'il. He reintroduced the "sadr" (Arabic *sadr*, leader), an office that had already existed in a similar form in the time of the Timurids and that was responsible for supervising religious institutions and endowments. With a view to transforming Iran into a Shi'ite state, the sadr was also assigned the task of disseminating Twelver doctrine and defending its dogma against unorthodox deviations. The office of the sadr thus served as a counterweight to the unorthodox fanaticism of the Kizilbash, who still venerated Isma'il's successor Tahmasp. When orthodox Twelver doctrine was finally established in the country, the office of sadr lost its political importance, whereas the influence of Twelver legal scholars, the mujtahids, grew.

The Arabic word *ijtihad* (lit. "exerting oneself") refers to the individual deduction of legal rules on the basis of intellectual reasoning. The principles underlying Twelver *ijtihad* were outlined during the Mongol periods by the scholar Al-'Allama (Arabic "the greatly learned") al-Hilli (1250-1325), who was active in Hilla, in southern Iraq, which was at that time the center of Twelver Shi'ite learning. In his view, only scholars possess the ability to arrive at valid knowledge by means of rational reflection, and they must have completed the appropriate course of training for this purpose. However, the mujtahid—that is, a scholar who practices *ijtihad*—is fallible, because only the twelfth imam can claim to be infallible. So long as the latter remains hidden, all results at which scholars arrive by means of reasoning are only provisional, so that the juxtaposition of contradictory decisions can be tolerated. Moreover, the mujtahid may not appeal to or cite an already deceased colleague, because each generation is supposed to come through discussion to its own consensus regarding the questions it faces. This conception of rational *ijtihad*, which was definitively developed in Twelver Shi'ism during the eighteenth century, establishes the authority of the mujtahid in matters of religion and law and thus provides the basis for the increasing influence—which was also political—of Twelver scholars.

The Safavids, especially Shah 'Abbas I and his court dignitaries, arranged extensive endowments for the benefit of Shi'ite holy places and institutions; Shi'ite scholars managed these endowments and drew revenue directly from them. Since according to Islamic law such endowments are inalienable and valid until Judgment Day, large amounts of money that accumulated from income on these endowments—as well as from the exercise of well-paid religious offices—passed into the hands of the mujtahids. The Shi'ite shrines in Mashhad and Qum, as well as the tombs of the imams in Iraq—Najaf, Karbala, Kazimayn, and Samarra—flourished anew. The endowed wealth of all these sites has continued to grow immeasurably through donations and endowments made either by the rulers of Iran or by believers throughout the world.

The increasing power of the mujtahids inevitably proved to be a threat to the position of the Safavid shahs. Like the shahs, the mujtahids claimed to be the sole legitimate representatives of the hidden imam. Although until the end of the Safavid dynasty the monarchy was strong enough to assert its role as the leader of the Shi'ah, the scholars' influence grew significantly under Shah 'Abbas's successors, most of whom were incompetent. It is true that there were periods when tensions declined, and when there was even a certain collaboration between rulers and scholars, but principally the mujtahids called the shah's authority into question. When the Safavid Empire came to an end, so did the only dynasty that could claim the aura connected with descent from the Prophet by way of the seventh imam and the authority to lead the Shi'ite community. The disappearance of this rival made the scholars an important power factor opposing the autocratic rule of later dynasties and providing a rallying point for all opponents of the monarchy. Furthermore, the final military loss of Iraq in 1639, which helped Shi'ite shrines located in Iran itself, such as Mashhad and Qum, gain new prestige, also favored the clergy's growing independence from the monarchy. When conflicts arose, the scholars could now evade the shah's immediate power by establishing themselves in one of the Shi'ite holy places in Iraq. In 1979, the mujtahids finally abandoned the role of opposition to the monarchy that they had occupied since the seventeenth century by overthrowing the shah and seizing power themselves. In this respect Iran is unique, since no Sunni country has ever undergone a similar development.

Iran in the Eighteenth Century

The Afghan invasion of Iran in 1722, which put an end to

the Safavid dynasty, was beaten back by Nadir Khan of the Turkmen tribe of Afshar. The Afshars, who had been members of the Kizilbash, lived a nomadic life in northern Khurasan. Nadir (b. 1688) was a military adventurer who spent his life in an almost unbroken series of wars and campaigns of conquest. Having begun his career as a military commander in the service of Safavid pretenders to the throne, in 1736 Nadir finally had himself crowned in the Mughan steppe in northwest Iran and henceforth took the name of Nadir Shah (reigned 1736-1747). He moved his capital city from Isfahan to Mashhad in Khurasan, which lay within the pastureland area of the Afshar tribe. His many military campaigns—through which he conquered large parts of Afghanistan, brought back from India the Peacock Throne and the famous Kohinoor diamond (from Persian *kuh-i nur*, "mountain of light") in 1739, and in 1746 re-established the border between Iran and the Ottoman Empire that had been set by the 1639 treaty of Zuhab— required enormous expenditures to maintain his huge army and in the long run depleted the country's resources. The inevitable consequence—oppressively higher taxes—soon made Nadir hated by the majority of those who felt the squeeze.

In particular, Nadir Shah's religious policies alienated the Twelver clergy when he tried to declare that the Twelver Shi'ism was a fifth school of law on an equal footing with the four already established orthodox Sunni law schools; he named it Ja'fariyya, after the Twelvers' sixth imam, Ja'far. This adaptation of a Sunni institution could not but arouse the opposition of the Shi'ite clergy. What they saw as Nadir

Shah's attempt to reintroduce Sunnism in Iran (in which the shah himself may have seen an opportunity to ease tensions with the Ottoman Empire and destroy the influential position of the Shi'ite clergy) succeeded only in driving many members of the clergy out of the country. They considered the shah's action to be a form of religious persecution and established themselves near the holy Shi'ite tombs in Ottoman Iraq. In the summer of 1747 Nadir Shah was murdered by a group of leading members of the Afshar and Qajar tribes.

Nadir Shah's death threw northern and northeastern Iran into chaos, with numerous military leaders fighting for power and territory. Only southern Iran, ruled by the Zand dynasty, experienced a period of peace and prosperity. The Zands came from the Iranian nomadic tribe of the same name, which lived in the central Zagros Mountains. One of their leaders, Muhammad Karim Beg, who was later known as Karim Khan and was one of the dynasty's most important rulers, reigned as a *wakil* (Arabic "deputy," "authorized representative"), initially as the deputy of the Safavid prince Isma'il III (reigned 1750-1753), whom he held in honorable imprisonment until his death in 1773. After Isma'il III's demise, Karim Khan did not install another puppet king, so that the idea of a possible restoration of the Safavid dynasty was finally abandoned. When he moved to Shiraz, which he made his capital at the beginning of the 1760s, Karim Khan changed his title to wakil al-ra'aya ("regent for the people").

After seven hundred years of Turkish and Mongol domination, the Zands were the first dynasty of Iranian descent. Their state, which lasted only a short time (1751-1794), brought peace and economic growth to southern Iran, especially under the rule of Karim Khan (reigned 1751-1779). Karim did not engage in unnecessary, ruinous wars of conquest and sought successfully to bring order and a certain level of prosperity to his devastated and impoverished country by imposing moderate taxes and reviving trade. The Zands claimed no religious authority, but in contrast to Nadir Shah they again encouraged Twelver Shiʿism. Each of the twelve districts of Shiraz was dedicated to one of the twelve imams, and the religious courts that had been abolished by Nadir Shah were reintroduced. Shiraz flourished anew as a trade and cultural center in which Karim Khan undertook an active building program that gave the city much of its present-day character. Among other things, he restored the memorials to the famed poets Saʿdi and Hafiz.

After Karim Khan died in 1779 his four sons immediately became instruments serving the ambitions of his relatives. By 1789 almost all male successors and relatives had either died in battle against each other or been executed, so that within a few years the country fell under the rule of the Turkish Qajar dynasty.

CHAPTER IV

From the Qajars to the Islamic Republic (1779 to the Present)

Demonstration for Khomeini

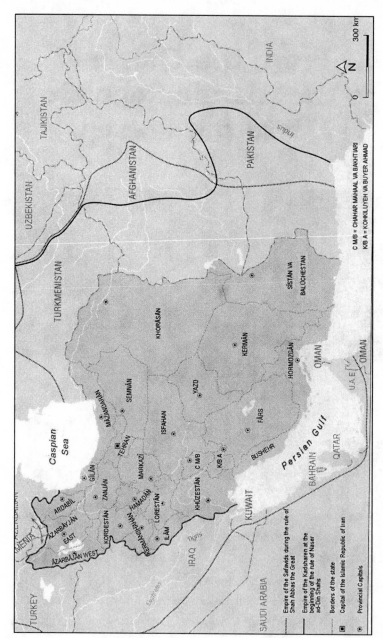

Iran in modern times

The Qajars

The history of the nineteenth century is shaped essentially by the massive expansion of the great European nations that pursued their competing colonial interests in the extra-European world by political and economic means. Inevitably, Iran was drawn into these conflicts: the Qajar dynasty (1779-1925), which had reunited Iran after the fall of the Safavid Empire and made it an important power in the Middle East, carried on a constant battle to maintain the country's political sovereignty and to preserve its territory. In the long run, however, the Qajars were unable to prevent either continuing territorial losses or the Europeans' increasing economic penetration of Iran. The military and technical superiority of Europe had become only too clear; this led to reflection on internal reforms whose urgency and necessity had become obvious, but also to stormy debates about the adoption of European secular ideas of the state and nation. The violent dispute that then began over Iran's adaptation to Western civilization, the danger of excessive Westernization, and a return to Iran's own traditional values continued unabated into the twentieth century.

Shah ʿAbbas I had resettled the Turkmen tribe of the Qajars, which belonged to the Kizilbash, along the northern border of Iran, which it was supposed to guard against attacks from the outside. After Karim Khan's death in 1779, Agha Muhammad, the son of a Qajar leader, was able to flee to northern Iran, win the support of the Qajar tribal groups there, bring most of the northern provinces under his control, and put an end to the Zands' rule in southern Iran. After he had conquered Azerbaijan, Armenia, and Georgia, in the spring of 1796 he had himself crowned as shah in the Mughan steppe; by assuming the old Persian title of *shahanshah* he also connected himself and the dynasty he founded—as many rulers before him had done—with the long Iranian tradition of kingship. Since the Qajars could claim no religious legitimation, Agha Muhammad strove to make his coronation an act of legitimation by using the ceremony that had been customary under the Safavids, thereby seeking to associate himself with the religious aura that surrounded them. A few years earlier, Agha Muhammad had already chosen as his capital Tehran, a provincial city near ancient Rayy, because it was close to the Qajar tribe's pasturelands southeast of the Caspian Sea. However, Tehran first began to grow significantly under Nasir od-Din (reigned 1848-1896), who, inspired by his travels in Europe, made the city into a genuine metropolis.

The foreign policy goal of the Qajar dynasty was to restore the borders of Iran as they had been under the Safavids, but they were unable to achieve this. Agha Muhammad was still able to conquer without great difficulty the province of Khurasan. However, after he was murdered in the summer of 1797 by two of his servants, his unworldly nephew Fath ʿAli Shah (reigned 1797-1834), who succeeded him on the throne, suffered considerable territorial losses. During his reign the European powers began to intervene directly in the internal affairs of Iran. Toward the end of the eighteenth century, Great Britain and Russia were the European nations with the greatest influence in the Middle East. During the whole of the nineteenth century they battled for military and economic predominance in Iran, which directly involved the interests of both countries: whereas Russia wanted to enlarge its national territory in the Caucasus, Great Britain wanted to acquire a land route to its Indian colonial possessions and keep Russia out of the Indian Ocean. The course of the war between Iran and Russia, which had annexed Georgia in 1801 and in 1804 advanced into Iranian territory in the Transcaucasus, was in large measure determined by the changing alliances among France, Great Britain, and Russia during the Napoleonic wars. As a consequence of these changing alliances, which the Iranians found unfathomable, the country lost large areas in the Caucasus that ultimately fell to Russia by the 1813 treaty of Golestan. Urged by the Shiʿite clergy to defend Muslims living in the Caucasus, the shah got involved in another war with Russia (1826) that ended in 1828 with the treaty of Turkmanchay (in Iranian Azerbaijan) and resulted, through the loss of further Caucasian provinces, in the establishment of the present-day border. In 1813 Iran had already been forced to accept the humiliating provision that future heirs to the Iranian throne would have to be endorsed by Russia. Now it was made to pay enormous damages and grant Russia full consular jurisdiction over Russian citizens in Iran, who were thereby completely exempted from Iranian legal authority. The notorious system of "capitulations," as they were called, which originated in this situation, was later expanded to include other European and Ottoman citizens in Iran as well.

In Nadir Shah's time, Iran's borders with the Ottoman Empire remained relatively stable, despite frequent tensions, but a definitive determination of its eastern border was not achieved until the middle of the nineteenth century. After unsuccessful attempts (1833, 1837) to reconquer Herat and western Afghanistan—formerly Iranian territory—Nasir al-Din undertook a new advance and seized Herat in the spring of 1856. The conflict that then broke out with Great Britain, which regarded Afghanistan as an indispensable buffer for its Indian colonies, ended in the 1857 treaty of Paris, by which Iran was forced to give up Herat and recognize the independence of Afghanistan. In 1872, through British mediation, the province of Sistan was divided between Iran and Afghanistan. Thereafter, the country's borders were, with few exceptions, those of present-day Iran.

The impression of Iran's unquestionable military inferiority led to the insight that if the country was to resist the European powers' threat effectively, reforms would have to be made. As in the Ottoman Empire, in Iran it was primarily the army that was to be transformed in accord with Western standards. At the beginning of the nineteenth century, Crown Prince ʿAbbas Mirza (1789-1833), the governor of Azerbaijan and one of the most enthusiastic advocates of reform, made great efforts to bring French and British military instructors to Iran, and at the same time to send Iranians to study in Europe. However, because they were not supported by the shah and the leading government dignitaries, his plans did not produce any decisive effect.

The reformers who vigorously pursued ʿAbbas Mirza's efforts were for the most part men who had come into contact with Western ideas while traveling in Europe. Among them was Nasir al-Din's prime minister, Emir Kabir (Mirza Taqi Khan, 1807-1851), who during his short term in office engaged in an energetic activity of reform, though once again primarily in the military sector. His efforts soon aroused the hostility of the bureaucracy and the court, resulting in his dismissal and eventual execution. In order to educate personnel capable of modernizing the army, he had founded in Tehran the polytechnic school *Dâr al-Fonûn* (Persian "school of the new sciences"), the first and for a long time the only institution of higher learning in Iran. In addition to military studies, it offered, under the guidance of foreign teachers, curricula in the natural sciences, medicine, and other areas, and thus abandoned the traditional theological studies in favor of European subjects (known as *fann*, plural *fonûn*, lit. "art, branch of knowledge"). The education provided by the new schools, in which European books were translated into Persian and Persian textbooks were written, thus disseminated European ideas and over time led to the development of a new class of intellectuals who had been influenced by Western ideas. Except for the *Dâr al-Fonûn*, none of the attempts at reform made during Nasir al-Din's long reign were able to move beyond their initial stages for lack of the financial means to carry them out. Only a Cossack brigade composed of Iranian, Turk, and other troops commanded by Russian officers was set up (1879); as long as it existed, it was the most powerful force in the Iranian army.

Iranian students and travelers who had resided for a considerable length of time in Europe—even if for the time being there were not many of them—made European political and legal structures and technical advancements known to a broader public in Iran. Their reports led to a new literary genre, travel memoirs. In addition to the translation of an increasing number of European books on various subjects, the new media of the telegraph and the printing press (the first one was set up in Tabriz in 1812, the second in Tehran in 1824) helped spread Western ideas. In the context of the expanded diplomatic contacts with the West that had been established since the beginning of the nineteenth century, Nasir al-Din was the first Iranian monarch to visit Europe; altogether, he made three such trips, leaving behind interesting travel journals.

The hesitation to undertake truly fundamental and cer-

tainly costly, but nonetheless necessary, reforms characterized the unsystematic modernization policies of the Qajar
rulers throughout the nineteenth century. In comparison
with the Ottoman Empire, efforts to implement reform in
Iran were far less frequent and more hesitant. The reason for
this—apart from the attitude of the shahs themselves, who
feared losing their power and having to make large expenditures—may be found above all in Iran's social structure, in
which the tribal leaders, the great landowners, and the clergy enjoyed greater independence than in other Islamic countries and, like the corrupt bureaucracy, vehemently defend-
ed their own interests.

The growing discontent with Iran's political dependence
on foreign powers and the increasing economic selling-out
of the country provoked, in the final years of Nasir al-Din's
reign, a protest movement in which conservatives and mod-
ernists joined in resisting the government and that finally led
to the Constitutional Revolution (1905-1911). The shah had
already been assassinated by a dissident in 1896.

The Qajar State

The Qajars saw themselves, as their title *shahanshah* clearly
indicated, as associated with the ancient Iranian tradition of
kingship. At the same time, the Qajars considered themselves the successors of the Safavids, whose administrative
structure they adopted. As absolute ruler, the shah stood
above all state officials, but he nonetheless ceded them the

power to make the real political decisions. However, the dependency of government officials on the shah and the ensuing insecurity of their positions induced them to strive to enrich themselves during their terms of office, constantly plotting against each other and attempting to retain their positions with the help of foreign powers, again particularly Great Britain and Russia.

From the outset, the Qajars were confronted by financial problems resulting from wars, weapons purchases, and the growing consumption of Western luxury goods, and these problems made repeated tax increases necessary, so that the situation of the rural population steadily deteriorated. Instead of establishing a regularly paid bureaucracy, the Qajars auctioned off public offices—such as those of customs officials and provincial governors—to the highest bidders. In turn, the officials who received high posts in this way leased out subordinate posts. The set sums of money that the governors were required to send annually to the capital, as well as those needed to finance the provincial administration and the governors' own often extravagant lifestyle, were collected on the spot. Provincial officials' nearly complete military and financial independence encouraged them to exploit their subjects, inciting ambitious types to rebellion and, given the lack of state control, leading local tribal leaders and major landowners to levy excessive taxes on the inhabitants of their own estates.

The West's political influence was accompanied by the European powers' attempts to make Iran economically dependent on them as well, and by demanding concessions, to gain control over at least part of the Iranian economy at low cost. The Iranian state's persistent liquidity problems made it easier to carry out this "peaceful" economic penetration of Iran, which by the end of the nineteenth century was headed for bankruptcy. After concessions for the construction of a telegraph network were granted to Great Britain in the 1860s, in 1872 the British citizen Julius de Reuter received a very far-reaching concession that put large parts of the Iranian economy under his control; however, in the following year pressure exerted by conservative groups, and especially by Russia, forced the shah to rescind this concession. For some time afterward, continuing rivalry between the two European powers providing "development aid," Great Britain and Russia, prevented the granting of further concessions that had been planned for the construction of a railway network. Only in 1879 did Russia acquire fishing rights in the Caspian Sea; additional concessions were awarded in the early 1880s. Toward the end of that decade, requests for concessions were piling up: the previously mentioned Baron Reuter received, through the mediation of the British envoy Sir Henry Drummond Wolff, permission to set up the Imperial Bank of Persia in Tehran — which, despite its name, was under British control. As a countermove, in 1890 the Russians were allowed to open their own credit bank, which later became a branch of the State Bank of Russia.

These unscrupulous concessions reached their apex in

March 1890, when the Imperial Tobacco Corporation of Persia, which was controlled by a British consortium, was granted a fifty-year monopoly on the production, purchase, and export of all Iran's tobacco. This concession was initially kept secret, but when toward the end of the year it became generally known, it provoked a mass protest. A religious edict (*fatwa*) issued in December 1891 and attributed to one of the leading Shi'ite scholars, Mirza Muhammad Hasan Shirazi, which declared any use of tobacco to be an offense against the hidden twelfth imam, led to a complete tobacco boycott throughout the country. As a result, the tobacco concession was rescinded in early 1892, and shortly thereafter another religious edict—of which this Shirazi was clearly the author—declared that the use of tobacco was now allowed again. However, the real importance of the conflict over the tobacco monopoly lies in the fact that here, for the first time in modern Iranian history, a successful mass movement came into being in which the clergy, the urban middle class, and intellectuals oriented toward modernity joined together in opposing the government and thereby made it clear how much influence such an alliance could have on the leadership of the state.

Shi'ism in the Nineteenth Century

During the nineteenth century, the Shi'ite clergy were able to increase their independence from the state. Since the Qajars lacked the religious legitimacy that the Safavids had enjoyed, the mujtahids considered them purely worldly rulers who did not have the religious authority that they themselves claimed. In addition, since the eighteenth century many clerics lived outside Iran in the Shi'ite holy places in Iraq and received revenues from endowments, donations, and so on. In modern times, the Shi'ite shrines in Iraq had become important centers of Shi'ite scholarship—and also centers of Shi'ite agitation. From these bases the mujtahids rigorously advocated their view that only the limited circle of specially trained scholars was qualified to make—by means of individual logical deduction—valid, authoritative decisions in religious matters, decisions that ordinary believers were required to accept without question (Arabic *taqlid*, lit. "imitate," i.e., submission to or acceptance of authority). Moreover, according to their own doctrine, which was definitively formulated in the Qajar period, only the mujtahids, as the deputies of the hidden imam, were qualified to perform the latter's functions until he returned. The mujtahids and their theory were ultimately able to prevail over all competing intra- and extra-Shi'ite religious movements, whether those of traditionalists who held that every believer was able to fulfill his own religious duties adequately without guidance by scholars, or those based on Sufi or Gnostic speculations, which did not recognize the authority of the mujtahids in religious matters. After the middle of the nineteenth century, with the emergence of a supreme theological authority, the clerical hierarchy assumed its present form. A particularly outstanding, exemplary scholar who was gener-

ally recognized within the clergy could be seen by his colleagues as the highest religious authority, as *marja'-e taqlid*
(Arabic *marji' al-taqlid*, "source of emulation" or "model for
reference"), but who is nonetheless fallible, like every mujtahid. This rank can be assigned to a single mujtahid or to
several simultaneously—or to no one, since there are not
always enough respected scholars who can be considered a
mardsha. The title of mardsha is an honorary title that may
be offered to a scholar, but not—for lack of an authorized
institution—formally conferred upon him.

In view of the European powers' increasing intervention
in internal Iranian affairs, especially in the economic sphere,
the clergy acquired a somewhat "national" role: that of the
protectors of the Iranian people's interests against foreign
influences, on the one hand, and against the Qajar shahs'
granting of concessions and their attempts to modernize the
country on the other. The clergy thus represented a strongly
conservative element in the society that saw itself as opposing, for the sake of Iran and of Islam, the influence of the
West as well as the worldly power of the monarchy; and this
was precisely the role that the mujtahids also played in the
twentieth century under the Pahlavi dynasty. Since the age of
the Safavids, in which state promotion of trade and industry
led to a significant increase in the number of craftsmen in
urban bazaars (*bazar*), a particularly close connection between these craftsmen and the clergy could be observed.
Often the clergy came from the social stratum of these
bazaar craftsmen, with whom they shared a common inter-

est in resisting foreign control over whole sectors of the economy—an alliance that still exists and in the modern history of Iran has more than once been an important determinant of the course of events.

Around the middle of the nineteenth century Shiʿism underwent a period of religious unrest during which new religious directions were established. The "Shaykhis," named after their founder, Shaykh Ahmad al-Ahsaʾi (1754-1826), were a group that had its roots in Twelver Shiʿism and who maintained that there must always be a man in the world who is capable of communicating with the hidden imam, and who can know and interpret the latter's will at all times. Under the influence of this movement, the theology student Sayyid Ali Muhammad (1819-1850) declared himself to be this intermediary. He proclaimed himself as the *bab* (Arabic "door," "gate," i.e., to the hidden imam) and representative of the twelfth imam; later he even claimed to be the mahdi himself. The Babi movement rapidly won many followers, especially since the *bab* proclaimed a new social order that was divinely willed and would produce greater social equality. Babi revolts against the government were cruelly suppressed, and in 1850 the *bab* was executed. However, his successor, Mirza Yahya Nuri (c. 1830-1912), who took the title Subh-i azal (Persian, "dawn of eternity"), retained on a minority of the Babis (the Azali-Babis, today a small, dwindling group with about 2000 members). Most of the Babis followed Mirza's half-brother Bahaʾi Ullah (Arabic "divine splendor"), who in 1863 declared himself to be the spiritual reincarnation of the *bab* and further developed the latter's messianic teaching. The Baha'i community quickly grew and spread over all the continents. In Iran, the Baha'i were subjected, under the autocratic rule of the Pahlavi dynasty, to a series of repressive measures. In the Islamic Republic, which does not count the Baha'is among the officially recognized religious communities, its situation has once again drastically worsened.

From the Constitutional Revolution to the Pahlavis

In the events that culminated in the so-called Constitutional Revolution and the constitutional movement (Persian *mashrutiyat*) of 1905, Shi'ite scholars played, because of their social position, a leading role in the opposition to the new shah Muzaffar al-Din (reigned 1896-1907). The general protest against the absolutism of the monarchy and the continually growing foreign influence on Iran—which was still a bone of contention between Great Britain and Russia—united the clergy with secular elements and progressive intellectuals. In the 1880s, the Iranian intellectual Jamal al-Din al-Afghani had already called for religious and non-religious opponents of Western colonial expansion to join forces. Al-Afghani greatly contributed to the spread of reformist ideas in Iran, including in religious milieus. More a political activist than a systematic thinker, throughout his life he propagated the idea of a spiritual—and not necessarily political—Islamic unity, the political cooperation of Muslims against overwhelming European superpowers, and an active, dynamic Islam. During two sojourns in Iran (1887, 1889-1891), al-Afghani gained influence over the younger generation of reform-minded Iranian intellectuals, whom he also introduced to the methods of organized resistance.

When the Iranian court's constant shortage of money—caused by the extravagant expenses incurred during the shah's stays at expensive European health spas—made it necessary to contract two large loans from Russia and forced new economic concessions, complete Russian control over Iran seemed dangerously near. Opposition to this development, which led to the founding of many secret societies comprising clerics and progressive secular thinkers, was stirred up by critical writings produced by expatriate Iranians. As a result of these writings, many who had up to that point never had an opportunity to visit other countries gained a new perspective on the conditions in Iran. Revolutionary feeling was strengthened by the victory of Japan, a country that had until recently been technically backward, over the great power Russia in early 1905, as well as by the Russian revolutionary uprising that had begun shortly thereafter. Starting in December 1905, this climate led to months of unrest in the course of which the original demand for representative institutions administering justice (using the vague Persian expression *'adalatkhaneh*, "house of justice") escalated into a call for a new constitution. Muzaffar al-Din was eventually compelled to consent to the election of a parliament (Persian *majlis*), and in October 1906 the latter actually convened. On December 30, shortly before he died, the shah signed the constitution (Persian *qanun-i asasi*), modeled largely on the Belgian constitution. The following year several amendments (Persian *motam-memât*) to the constitution were drafted and signed by Muzaffar al-Din's successor, Muhammad Ali Shah (reigned 1907-1909). The absolute monarchy that had ruled Iran since time immemorial was thereby transformed into a constitutional monarchy in which the ministers were no longer accountable to the shah but to the parliament. This weakening of the monarchy benefited the Shiʿite clergy more than it did the progressive forces familiar with Western ideas that had fought for the democratization of Iran. An amendment to the constitution passed in 1907 provided that all parliamentary decisions should be submitted to a committee of five Shiʿite clerics which was to evaluate their compatibility with Islamic law (Shariʿah). This amendment meant that the mujtahids could now revise all proposed laws in accord with their own views or even block them altogether.

The new form of government in Iran was short-lived, because it brought the country neither stability nor progress; above all, financial problems persisted. In 1907, in order to settle their mutual differences in Asia, Great Britain and Russia signed a treaty dividing Iran into three areas corresponding to their spheres of interest: the northern zone was assigned to Russia and the southern to Great Britain, with a neutral buffer zone separating them. Muhammad Ali used a failed attempt to assassinate him as a pretext for suppressing the parliament with the help of the Persian Cossack Brigade and for suspending freedom of the press. Rebellions flared up in the provinces, especially in northwest Iran, that forced the shah to abdicate before the year was out. His son Ahmad (reigned 1909-1925) was still a minor, but he was nonetheless designated as the new ruler by the rebels and was recognized by Great Britain and Russia. In 1911, in order to resolve Iran's persistent budgetary problems, the government—whose previous experiences with Great Britain and Russia had led it to mistrust both these nations—hired the American expert William Morgan Shuster to reorganize the government's finances. Shuster's plan to have taxes collected by special police units headed by an officer of the British Indian Army aroused Russia's protest. When the parliament refused to dismiss Shuster and Russian troops advanced toward Teheran, the regent, Nasir al-Mulk, who administered the government's affairs on behalf of the still-underage shah, dissolved the parliament and fired Shuster. Nonetheless, Russia continued to occupy areas of northern Iran and, in conjunction with Great Britain, saw to it that press censorship remained in force and that a parliament acceptable to the two countries was installed. This put a de facto end to the Constitutional Revolution as well; the constitution was suspended.

In the First World War, Iran officially declared its neutrality, but the latter was not respected by the great powers. Russia, the Ottoman Empire, and Britain all fought battles on Iranian soil, with the result that the central government almost completely collapsed and the country was thrown into chaos. The Russian revolution in October 1917 found many sympathizers in Iran, especially since the new Bolshevik government promised henceforth to respect Iran's territorial sovereignty. Thus after the Russian troops' withdrawal from Iran, Great Britain remained the only militarily and economically significant power in the Middle East. In 1919, after the failure of its attempt to make Iran a kind of British protectorate, Great Britain changed its policy and began to support the installation of a strong Iranian central government that could establish internal order and at the same time ward off the threat of expansion on the part of the new Soviet Union. Therefore Britain welcomed it when in February 1921 Reza Khan, an officer in the Persian Cossack Brigade, staged a coup d'etat and installed a new premier. As minister of war in the new government, Reza Khan reorganized the army and put down rebel movements in the provinces of Azerbaijan, Gilan, and Khuzistan. By means of a second coup d'etat carried out in 1923, he made himself prime minister and was able to get through a series of laws that strengthened the central government: compulsory military conscription, the standardization of weights and measures throughout the country, the introduction of family names and birth certificates, and the use of revenues from the state tea and sugar monopoly for the construction of a Trans-Iranian railroad.

In spring 1925 the parliament decided to depose the last

Qajar ruler, Ahmad (who had left Iran in 1923 to travel in Europe), and to transform itself into a constitutional assembly that in December 1925 finally agreed to raise Reza Khan to the throne as the new shah. Thus began the short-lived Pahlavi dynasty (1925-1979)—named after the language of pre-Islamic Iran, Pahlavi. Ahmad Shah never returned to his country.

The Pahlavis

Backed by the army he had modernized, Reza Shah reigned as a despot, so that the parliament, which formally approved the decisions he made, was no more than a kind of democratic veneer. In contrast to the time of the Qajars, during which only a few effective reforms were introduced, Reza Shah's primary goal was to make Iran into a progressive, secular nation-state on the European model by means of a large-scale program of modernization such as Atatürk, whom he greatly admired, had set underway in Turkey. From his coronation to his abdication in 1941, the shah implemented the first truly significant series of effective reforms and undertook to create a functioning infrastructure: the Trans-Iranian railroad from the Persian Gulf to Tehran and the northern provinces was built (1926-1938) and rapidly advancing road construction made motor vehicles the main means of transportation between small towns and villages. The development of agriculture and industry was intensified and the legal system secularized on European models through new legal codes (Commercial Code, 1925; Criminal Code, 1926; Civil Code, 1928), as was the educational system. A network of public elementary schools was established, and in Tehran the first modern university in Iran opened in 1935; Iranians were also encouraged to study abroad. Western-style clothing for men was made obligatory in 1929; in 1936 it was also made obligatory for women, and the wearing of the veil was prohibited. However, the prohibition of the veil could not be enforced even by coercion, so that after 1941 women, especially lower-class women, began to wear it again. Muharram celebrations were forbidden, and the professional activities of the clergy restricted to the religious realm alone; only the clergy was allowed to retain its traditional clothing (caftan and turban), so that it was now also defined outwardly as a separate social group. All these measures had the effect of banishing Islam from public life and undermining the position of the clergy.

The beneficiaries of the modernization of Iran undertaken by Reza Shah were the steadily growing governmental bureaucracy, which was used to keep watch over the state, the new entrepreneurs who profited from increasing industrialization, and the great landowners, since land reform did not take place and the provisions of the new Civil Code were undermined by bribery and personal connections. On the other hand, industry and the countless construction sites throughout the country required a more mobile labor force, so that workers were often forced to abandon their traditional ways of life. Social transformation manifested itself with particular clarity in the immense growth of the cities, in which large numbers of peasants—drawn to the cities by the promise of better living conditions—constituted a steadily expanding proletariat.

In order to create a strong central government, Reza Shah considered it urgently necessary to sedentarize the often more or less independent and well-armed nomadic tribes, which constituted about one fourth of the total population, the better to control them. After his power was sufficiently established, the shah began in 1927 a rigorous policy of sedentarizing the nomads, who were forcibly disarmed and compelled to settle the areas that had been designated for them—which were often unsuitable for keeping livestock. Thus the nomads' herds were prevented from making the necessary migrations between summer and winter pastures, so that many animals died. In addition to this economic disaster, health problems emerged due to the malarial diseases that often broke out during the summer and which the tribes' earlier migrations had spared them. Tribal resistance was ruthlessly put down by the army, and most tribal leaders were executed or expelled.

Reza Shah's foreign policy sought to present his country to the international public as an independent nation-state. To this end the Pahlavis attempted to return, as the name of their dynasty indicates, to Iran's pre-Islamic past; from the outset, at his coronation, the shah made this new nationalism evident by having his crown and banner made in the

Sasanian style and by wearing a cloak imitating the ancient Iranian model. In 1934, the official name of the country was no longer to be the European "Persia," but rather "Iran." In 1927-28, the shah canceled nearly all Iran's agreements with foreign states insofar as they infringed on the equality of the parties, and abolished the humiliating concessions. Seeking to make Iran as independent of Great Britain and Russia as possible, Reza Shah had, after attempts to establish closer relations with the United States had failed, turned increasingly to Germany. Nonetheless, in the Second World War Iran tried to remain neutral, but once again it was unable to assert its own interests against those of the great powers. In August 1941 British and Soviet troops marched into Iran, forced the shah to abdicate, and deported him to South Africa, where he died in 1944. His son Muhammad Reza Shah (1941-1979) succeeded him on the throne with the approval of the occupying powers.

The new shah (b. 1919) cooperated with the Allies and in 1943 was recognized by treaty as an ally, but until the occupation ended in 1946 his freedom of action remained restricted. At first, Muhammad Reza endorsed the constitutional monarchy, but during these years the parliament essentially paralyzed itself by engaging in partisan factional struggles. Taking advantage of weakness of the young shah, various social-revolutionary movements that had been repressed by Reza Shah fused in the communist Tudeh party (Persian *tudeh*, "masses"); many nomadic tribes reorganized themselves and went back to their traditional way of life, and the clergy also sought to regain influence. The Muharram celebrations were gradually resumed, and in 1948 a religious edict (*fatwa*) issued by one of the leading mujtahids declared that women once again had a duty to wear the veil.

Shortly thereafter the shah found himself involved in serious conflicts with Premier Muhammad Mosaddeq, who was the head of the National Front, a coalition of liberal and religious nationalist parties. His attempt to nationalize the Anglo-Iranian Oil Company, in which Great Britain held a majority stock position and which was considered by many Iranians to be a channel for British influence in the country, ended—as a result of pressure exerted by both Britain and the United States—in a boycott of Iran by almost all the major oil companies, and the ensuing decrease in oil revenues had a damaging effect on the state's finances. During this crisis, in which Mosaddeq had to rely on the support of the Tudeh party, the shah fled abroad, returning later in the same year after Mosaddeq had been overthrown in a coup staged by the army. The American CIA played a role in this coup, in an attempt to prevent Iran from establishing closer ties with the Soviet Union. After Mosaddeq's fall, the oil problem was settled by an agreement to apportion oil revenues to a consortium of several international oil companies and the National Iranian Oil Company. The latter's share of these revenues was henceforth considerably larger and further increased when new oil deposits were discovered near Ghom (1956).

Like Great Britain before them, during the Cold War the

United States was greatly interested in binding Iran to the Western allies in order to have a reliable bulwark against communism in the Middle East. As a result, the country received extensive American military aid that enabled the shah was able to modernize and enlarge his army. Again with foreign support, the shah set up an internal intelligence service (S.A.V.A.K.) that became active in 1957 and developed into an instrument of surveillance that was feared throughout the land. The army and the secret police were Muhammad Reza's main agents for enforcing his authority. After Mosaddeq's fall, the shah became more and more of a despot like his father, but without the latter's energy. Responding to American pressure, in 1960 Muhammad Reza began a short phase of liberalization during which the National Front was allowed to resume its activities, but in 1963 he once again shut down oppositional movements by force. As a result, not only were democratic structures eliminated, but also the idea of democracy suffered serious damage in Iran, because the West supported the shah's autocratic regime on grounds that were obviously connected with power politics. The shah himself willingly played the role of a "policeman of the Gulf," protecting Western and above all American interests. In 1975 the two authorized political parties, which in any case had only a shadowy existence, were dissolved and merged in a single party, *Rastakhiz* ("resurrection"), to which most adult citizens had to belong.

Iran's economic growth, which had been greatly accelerated by oil revenues and the influx of foreign capital, especially toward the end of the 1960s, not only resulted in significant governmental and private investment, but also contributed to the increasing prosperity of a previously small middle class that was now becoming larger, and which, under pressure from the S.A.V.A.K.—and perhaps sometimes not unwillingly—turned away from politics and devoted itself entirely to Western-style consumerism. However, since as a result of this economic development basic foodstuffs became more expensive and corruption increased, over time social tensions inevitably intensified. With the development program known as the "White Revolution" (Persian *inqilab-i safid*), Muhammad Reza thus undertook the first serious efforts at reform intended to improve the situation in rural areas. Although peasants received plots of land, they nonetheless remained for the most part dependent on the great landowners because they lacked the means to farm their land by themselves. This situation led to increased migration to the cities and to further growth of the urban proletariat. In addition to land reform, the shah set as his goal the establishment of the legal equality of men and women: in 1962, women were given active and passive voting rights, and a family protection law enacted in 1967 facilitated divorce initiated by women. Both these initiatives encountered resistance from the clergy because they feared the loss of their endowments, and also because they fundamentally rejected any tendencies toward Westernization.

In the 1960s and 1970s, the shah became increasingly alienated from his own people, although he did not seem to realize it. The preparations for the celebration in Persepolis of the twenty-five-hundredth anniversary of the Iranian monarchy (1971) were extremely extravagant in view of the living conditions of the majority of the people, the introduction of a new calendar (1976) that took the year of the coronation of the Achaemenid king Cyrus the Great (550 BC) as its starting point, and a planned international symposium intended to resolve the world's problems (1977), are all indications of Muhammad Reza's fragile grip on reality. He overlooked the fact that only a minority of the population had profited from economic growth, and that his policy of Westernization deeply offended many devout Iranians for whom their religion was a basic element of their identity. On the other hand, his extremely repressive internal policy forfeited the sympathies of Western-oriented Iranians, who could not imagine progress without democratic freedoms. Because there was no channel for political co-determination and criticism of the government, the religious opposition offered the only way to articulate resistance to the shah's autocratic rule. The Shi'ite clergy thus once again assumed its traditional role of defending the Iranian people against un-Islamic influences and a despotic government.

The true cause of the Islamic Revolution was thus the political, social, and economic crisis into which the shah had led his country, yet inevitably the religious element got the most attention. In the West, where the growing gulf between the clergy and the shah had in any case not been perceived, the religious justification for the revolution created the impression that it was nothing more than a deliberate "return to the Middle Ages." When in 1978 the swelling discontent broke out in a mass protest movement, the revolution could no longer be halted. In January 1979 the shah left Iran; he died of cancer in Cairo in 1980.

Political Shi'ism and the Islamic Revolution

In the West, the Islamic Revolution and the foundation of an Islamic Republic left the erroneous impression that Twelver Shi'ism had always been a politically revolutionary ideology. It is nothing of the sort. While Shi'sm's original goal was in fact to establish at the head of the Muslim community a legitimate successor of the Prophet, but when this aspiration was not fulfilled after 'Ali's caliphate, it could henceforth only be realized through the return of the hidden imam. Traditionally, therefore, Twelver Shi'ism had been unpolitical, even quietist; and with few exceptions its clergy has kept its distance from day-to-day politics. The idea of a politically active Shi'ism is a new phenomenon and sprang not from the learned clergy's ideas but rather from Iranian intellectuals who felt that Iran was infiltrated by foreign cultural domination and economically exploited. The men who paved the way for revolutionary ideology and shaped a whole generation of young Iranians were Jalal Al-i Ahmad (1923-1969) and his student 'Ali Shari'ahti (1933-1977).

Whereas up to that point Western models had remained authoritative for most Iranian intellectuals regardless of their political direction, even though their benefit for Iran was becoming increasingly doubtful, Al-e Ahmad induced them to return to their own cultural values. His best known work, *Gharbzadigi* (1952) provided the key to a worldview in which leftists and Islamists joined together in opposition to the shah's despotism and his obedience to the West. The title of Al-e Ahmad's—which has been translated as "attacked by the West," "poisoned by the West," and "Occidentential-tosis"—refers to the blind imitation of the West that was alienating the Iranian people from their own roots. Although personally inclined to nationalism, Al-e Ahmad saw religion as the only cultural value in Iran that had not yet been poisoned by the Westand that still remained of paramount importance for the majority of Iranians.

Shari'ahti, who had been educated in France and who shared Al-e Ahmad's convictions, also attacked the cultural "colonization" of Iran by the West. He developed the notion of a combative, dynamic Islam that he thought had been realized in the original Muslim community of Muhammad and 'Ali's era. Thus Shari'ahti imparted an entirely new quality to Twelver Shi'ism by drawing a sharp distinction between "Alid or red Shi'ism" and "Safavid or black Shi'ism." "Red Shi'ism" represents the original, uncorrupt-ed, true Shi'ism of the Golden Age at the beginning, which constitutes an active Islam, a progressive, revolutionary movement that stood up for justice and fought all kinds of foreign domination, oppression, arbitrary despotism, and exploitation. By making it the state religion, the Safavids

had reduced this Shi'ism—which had always opposed tyran-
ny—to a mere institution, a means of political enslavement.
"Black Shi'ism" is thus a depraved form of religious belief
that seeks to get along with worldly despots and exploiters
and has replaced holy martyrdom with the pathetic—
because wholly passive—mourning of the Muharram celebrations. The notion of a combative Alid Shi'ism thus freed
Shi'ism from the current petrified religious tradition and
obligated all believers to engage in political action. The new,
subversive content of this utopian Shi'ism expressed itself in
two incisive and in fact revolutionary reinterpretations of
traditional Shi'ite principles. Shari'ahti urged the whole population to act as representatives of the hidden imam and to
establish here and now the realm of justice as precisely this
imam had been expected to do in an eschatological future.
According to this conception, the mujtahids would lose
their superior position and their task would be limited to
organizing revolutionary movements. Second, according to
Shari'ahti, every place is Karbala, every month is Muharram, every day is 'Ashura—and this became one of the slogans of the Islamic Revolution. It means neither more nor
less than that the ritual of symbolic self-sacrifice that the
Shi'ites perform once a year on the day of 'Ashura should be
replaced by revolutionary war, and if necessary, by actual
martyrdom. Notwithstanding Shari'ahti's completely ahis-
torical perspective on the many past centuries of Islamic history, through belief in these ideas, traditionally unpolitical
Shi'ism was transformed into a revolutionary ideology that

was able to unite diverse oppositional groups that had been drawn together by their collective struggle against Western imperialism, and their hatred of the shah was its tool. In 1973, Shari'ahti was forbidden to speak in public and moved in 1977 to London, where he died the same year. The Islamic Revolution, of which both he and Al-e Ahmad may be considered the ideological forerunners, nonetheless ignored many of their originally anti-clerical and to some extent even Western-influenced ideas.

Ayatollah Ruhollah Khomeini (1902-1989) became the leader of the Islamic Revolution. "Ayatollah" (Arabic *ayat Allah*, "sign of God") is a high honorary title that can be attributed to a mujtahid. Khomeini came from a family of small landowners in the town of Khumayn (between Hamadan and Isfahan) that traced its ancestry back to the seventh imam, Musa al-Kazim. After completing his education, Khomeini became a close associate of Ayatollah Husayn Burujirdi in Qum, who was averse to engaging in any political activity. It was probably his influence that at first prevented Khomeini from taking public political positions. Only in June 1963, a year after Burujirdi's death, did Khomeini begin his direct attack on the shah; in a stirring speech he denounced the shah and the Iranian nouveaux riches as parasites on the body of the people, and openly called for resistance. In 1964, after twice being imprisoned, he was sent into exile in Turkey and finally settled in 1965 at the shrine of Najaf in Iraq, where he continued to teach and give sermons; tape recordings of his speeches, in which he called for the overthrow of the shah, circulated in great numbers and, disseminated by a well-functioning network of religious groups, elicited wide interest among the Iranian people. In October 1978, having been expelled from Iraq, Khomeini continued his propaganda activity against the shah from Neauphle-le-Château, near Paris. The fact, found astonishing by Westerners, that he was able to lead a successful revolution from such a distance can be explained if we reflect that the Shi'ite clergy had long since played oppositional roles from outside Iran; whether they did so from Najaf or Neauphle-le-Château is irrelevant.

Khomeini succeeded in calling forth in Iran a mass protest movement against the shah's dictatorship that—like the Constitutional Revolution—united a spectrum of diverse opposition groups: leftists and rightists, liberals and conservatives, intellectuals, bazaar merchants, radicals and moderate groups of clergy, as well as the great mass of impoverished former landowners now living in the slums of the great cities. These groups inevitably had different ideas about the future of Iran after the shah was overthrown. Khomeini succeeded in conveying the impression that he himself was only a rallying point and that after the revolution succeeded, he and his colleagues would return to their mosques and madrasahs without trying to establish a government. In order to maintain the external unity of the revolutionary movement, he at first avoided talking about his ideas regarding a theocratic state. Instead, he promised that the social system would be retained, with democratic freedoms and equal rights for men and women. This won him wide support, especially among Iranian women. Often these women were members of liberal or leftist groups who hoped for future democratic development in Iran, and saw the full body veil (*chadur*) as only a symbol of protest against the shah. The condition that Khomeini regularly added to his promises, namely that all this must be in accord with Islam, apparently was not sufficiently noticed. Only in the fall of 1978, at an advanced stage of the revolutionary movement, did Khomeini openly demand the establishment of an Islamic Republic.

The real trigger for the revolutionary events was a newspaper article that appeared in the government-controlled press on January 7, 1978 and that violently slandered Khomeini. This resulted in demonstrations staged by theology students that were brutally suppressed by the police. The clergy sharply condemned the government and its actions as un-Islamic, and ordered a period of mourning for the victims, during which there were further protests. A cycle of mass demonstrations, clashes with police and military forces, followed by new demonstrations, was repeated over and over. After the shah finally left Iran in January 1979, Khomeini flew on February 1 from Paris to Tehran, where he dissolved the civilian interim adminstrtion set up by the shah and called upon the devoutly religious engineer Mehdi Bazargan to form a provisional revolutionary government, thus putting an end to the revolution.

The Islamic Republic

A referendum in March 1979 proposing the establishment of an Islamic Republic was approved—as was foreseeable—by about 97 percent of the voters. The republic was officially proclaimed on April 1 and at the beginning of the following December its new constitution was endorsed by popular vote.

According to this constitution, the Islamic Republic is a theocracy in which God is the sole ruler. Until the hidden imam returns—and this is also part of the constitution—the basic principle of the "representative governance of the jurist" (Persian *vilayat-i faqih*), which Khomeini had developed in his book *Islamic Government* (Persian *Hukumat-i Islami*, 1971) is to be applied. In this work Khomeini stipulates that direct governmental power should be in the hands of the best qualified legal jurist (*fakih*) or, in case there is no generally recognized mujtahid, of a committee of jurists who are to rule as representatives of the hidden imam until the latter's return. This goes far beyond the function of supervising the government assigned to the clergy by the 1907 amendment to the constitution, and explicitly asserts the claim that only Shi'ite legal scholars are entitled to be legitimate representatives of the hidden imam. That the clergy's representative role would lead to the exercise of actual political power is no more foreseen in traditional Shi'ism than is the office of a supreme spiritual and political leader of the Khomeini type. Both are qualitatively new and so rev-

olutionized traditional Shi'ism that they long aroused conservative clerics to stubbornly resist such innovations.

By a plebiscite held in December 1979, Khomeini was
confirmed in the office, established in the constitution, of
supreme religious and political leader (Persian *rahbar*) of
Iran. In addition to a Supreme Leader or Leadership Council of Shi'ite jurists, the constitution provides for a Council
of Guardians composed of an equal number of religious
and secular jurists, and—resuming the tenor of the 1907
amendment to the constitution—entrusts it with the task of
ensuring that laws passed by the parliament are in accord
with Islam. Khomeini combined in his person the office of
political leader with the religious authority of a *marja'*.
However, since his successor would not necessarily have the
same rank, a 1989 amendment to the constitution separated
the office of the political leader from that of the religious
leader. The religious political leader, who is at the same time
the head of state, need no longer be a *mardsha*, and the current occupant of this office, Ali Khamene'i (b. 1940), is not
one. On the same occasion, the office of the prime minister
was abolished and the state president given the task of leading the government; the latter's position was thus significantly strengthened.

Shortly after the revolution, the differing political interests of the various groups that had lent their common support to the movement re-emerged. Nonetheless, Khomeini
succeeded in eliminating the moderate, liberal, and leftist
oppositional groups that rejected the clergy's seizure of

power, sidelining critical liberal clerics, and realizing his conception of a theocratic state. In particular, the leftist People's Mujahidin (Persian *Mojaihdin-i khalq*), which had been founded in 1965 as a group opposing the shah's government and which had largely contributed to the revolution's victory, carried on in the early 1980s guerrilla activities against the Islamic Revolutionary Guards Corps (IRGC) established by Khomeini, and made many assassination attempts. Two bomb attacks in June 1981 killed numerous figures who had been involved in the revolution. Now the clergy finally had their own revolutionary martyrs. The government responded to the Mujahidin's terrorist attacks with an even more comprehensive campaign of persecution that resulted in thousands of victims throughout the country, not only among the Mujahidin, but also among opposition and heterodox groups of all kinds, so that democratic protests such as strikes and demonstrations became virtually impossible until Khomeini's death. Thus after 1981 a theocratic state could be implemented. The clergy also took over the office of state president, which at first had been held by religious "laymen." After Mehdi Bazargan (d. 1995) retired from the office of prime minister in late 1979 as a result of disputes with the clergy about governmental responsibility, it came as a surprise when at the beginning of the following year Abu al-Hasan Bani-Sadr, one of Khomeini's advisors in Neauphle-le-Château, was elected the first state president of the republic. After his overthrow he fled to Paris. His successor in this office was Muhammad Ali Raja'i, a member of the Islamic Republican Party (IRP), which was loyal to Khomeini. Afterward this office was held by Ali Khamene'i (1981-1989), who in 1989 became Khomeini's successor, by Ali Akbar Rafsanjani (1989-1997), and Muhammad Khatami (1997-2005)—all three of them clerics. In 2005, in another presidential election surprise, the engineer Mahmud Ahmadinejad, a former mayor of Tehran, defeated Rafsanjani, who had been especially favored by the Western powers. He is the second Iranian state president, after Bani-Sadr, not to be a member of the clergy.

After the defeat of the opposition, the clergy tried—in the name of Islam, which it praised as the solution to any problem the country might have—to Islamize Iran's culture: penal law was implemented in conformity with Islamic religious law, women were again required to wear a veil, alcohol was prohibited; school textbooks were rewritten in accord with Islamic ideas and cookbooks were revised to comply with Qur'anic food regulations. Iraq's attack on Iran in September 1980, by which the Iraqi dictator Saddam Hussein hoped to gain control over the whole Shatt al-Arab area and the oil fields in Khuzistan, plunged Iran into an eight-year-long war that claimed countless victims on the Iranian side. However, the war made it easier for the government to impose tighter internal restrictions by appealing to the necessity of defeating the external enemy, against whom all the country's resources had to be mobilized. The significant restriction of freedom of speech, along with propaganda against a Westernized, "corrupt" elite, drove many members of the intelligentsia—about a million Iranians—to leave the country. This, combined with the closing of the universities that was connected with the war and lasted for years, seriously damaged Iranian art, culture, and science. Resentment against the West led Khomeini to issue in February 1989, shortly before his death, a fatwa in which he condemned the British writer Salman Rushdie to death because in his book *The Satanic Verses* Rushdie had satirized the life the Prophet. This fatwa, which Khamene'i repeated after Khomeini's death to give it continuing validity, led to a rupture of Iran's relations with Great Britain and did severe damage to its international reputation. Khomeini also contributed to the isolation of Iran, which began when Iranian students occupied the United States embassy in Tehran in 1979, by his propaganda against Israel, for whose destruction clerical leaders regularly called in speeches on domestic policy given on Jerusalem Day (the last Friday of the fasting-month of Ramadan). The repetition of this already formulaic demand by the current state president, Mahmud Ahmadinejad, on the foreign policy level is a new development that is regarded with increasing concern—not least, of course, by Israel.

Above all, Khomeini failed to prove that Iran's severe economic problems could be solved by Islamic leadership. It quickly became evident that a rapidly growing population and an increasing rural exodus could not be dealt with by religious slogans. In Tehran, the number of inhabitants rose from five to nine million during the decade 1979-1989, and by 1993 it had reached thirteen million. The war with Iraq ended in 1988 with a cease-fire that did not demand that the aggressor, Iraq, pay reparations. A few years earlier, when Iranian fighters had driven the Iraqi army back over the border, it would have been possible to negotiate such payments. But since at that time Khomeini himself had ordered that the war be continued, it was inevitable that people would eventually come to the bitter realization that many thousands of soldiers had died in vain on the battlefield.

After Khomeini's death in June 1989, Rafsanjani, who became state president when Khamene'i took over as supreme religious leader, tried to open Iran to foreign investment. This resulted in a large influx of products—for the most part financed by foreign loans—onto the Iranian market, but because the Islamic Republic was not trusted in matters of politics and the management of the economy, the desired long-term investments were not forthcoming. Instead, imports had to be drastically reduced, causing disturbances in many Iranian cities. Iran's economic problems still await solution.

In the area of domestic policy, the new state president counted on a careful liberalization of public and cultural life, for example by alleviating censorship of the press. However, Rafsanjani's policy suffered repeated setbacks because he had constantly to struggle against the predominance of the conservative clerics. In the mid-1990s, this conservative faction intensified their attacks on the easing of restrictions achieved by reform politicians. Consequently, censorship of the press was increased, writers and newspaper editors were arrested or fled, and the possession of satellite dishes was forbidden in order to cut off "un-Islamic" foreign influences.

Even under the liberal state president Khatami, who was elected in 1997 by a large majority, the conflicts between reformers and conservatives continued. Although Khatami was the first Iranian president to visit the West, and although parliamentary elections in the year 2000 gave supporters of reform a clear majority, true power remained for the most part in the hands of the religious leader, Khamene'i, who controls the police, the secret service, and the armed forces and who has the support of the council of Guardians. These power relationships were reflected in the 2004 parliamentary elections, in advance of which the council of Guardians excluded numerous candidates (about 2,500 out of 8,200), primarily on the ground that their convictions were not—or not sufficiently—Islamic. Moreover, since many reform-minded Iranians, chiefly members of the younger generation, did not vote as a protest against the exclusion of these candidates, the victory of the conservatives and their absolute majority in the parliament were assured. President Khatami's rather timid efforts on behalf reforms that the Iranian intelligentsia had long vehemently demanded thus remained for the time being unsuccessful.

Under the new president who has been in office since 2005, the radical-conservative Ahmadinejad, the trend toward a policy in strict accord with Islam has continued in accord with Ahmadinejad's campaign promise to realize the ideals of the 1979 revolution. This promise, along with promises to resolve Iran's social problems and provide food and work for everyone, won him the votes of the poorer classes as well as those of Iranians who rejected a Western orientation of their country.

However, less than two years later Ahmadinejad got the bill for his unfulfilled romises, especially in the social area: in local elections held in December 2006, his conservative opponents were very successful, and the forces of reform also made progress. Ahmadinejad's sponsor, Ayatollah Mesbah-e Yazdi, defeated his opponent, the supposedly moderate conservative Rafsanjani.

As for Ahmadinejad's foreign policy, the conflict regarding Iran's use of nuclear power has grown more intense during his term in office. The Iranian government insists that this conflict concerns only the peaceful use of nuclear energy, but it could also concern the production of nuclear weapons, and may become more acute in the future. In the 1980s Iran had already begun a nuclear program coordinated by Rafsanjani and further developed during his presidency. Understandably, the West is concerned about the uncontrolled proliferation of nuclear weapons, especially when they are in the hands of a regime that the West considers unpredictable. In the Iranian view, the international configuration of power requires Iran to be capable of effectively protecting itself against potential aggressors. Iran, which has not engaged in an aggressive war for more than a century and half but in the recent past has suffered under massive outside influence to the point of losing territory, currently sees itself—directly or indirectly—surrounded by nuclear powers (Israel, Pakistan, India, Russia, China) and American military bases (in Turkey, Afghanistan, and parts of the former Central Asian Soviet republics). In addition, the war conducted in Iraq by the United States and Great Britain since 2003 has led many Iranians to conclude that their country is surrounded on all sides by enemies and that it must be prepared to defend itself. Even President Khatami, who was seen in the West as a reformer, pursued a hard-line national foreign policy on this issue with respect to what seemed in Iran to be an arrogant intervention on the part of the West. Many Iranians, who reject the current regime, are inclined to back it on the nuclear issue because of their national patriotic feeling.

Women in Modern Iran

In Iran, the first movements toward equal rights for women, based on the unquestioned equality of men and women before God in Islam, go back to the turn of the twentieth century. They were triggered by the confrontation with Western ideas in the late nineteenth century, and at that time involved chiefly educated and influential women from the upper classes or the royal house. Thus, for example, many women from Nasir al-Din Shah's harem joined the tobacco boycott of 1890-1892. During the Constitutional Revolution of 1905-1911, champions of the women's movement, once again from the upper classes, organized themselves into groups and, supported by many male intellectuals, wrote newspaper and magazine articles advocating women's rights. However, under pressure from the clergy, most of the periodicals devoted to the women's movement had to suspend publication until about 1920. Nevertheless, between 1906 and 1910, again despite resistance from conservative clerics, about fifty schools for girls were opened in Tehran. Although up to that point all efforts to improve the lot of women had been based on private initiative, this situation radically changed under the Pahlavis. In 1935, under the rule of Reza Shah, a state-sponsored Women's Center (Persian *Qanun-i Banuvan*) was founded most of whose members had participated in the women's movement. The government was able to suppress by force the resulting outburst of clerical resistance, but it subsequently flared up again and again. As a counter-reaction, women's associations were established privately, as they had been before Reza Shah, and these associations pursued their goals by publishing periodicals advocating women' rights. Above all, female suffrage, which had been an issue ever since the Constitutional Revolution, was repeatedly demanded, but because of clerical resistance it was not granted until 1963, in the framework of the White Revolution. In 1966, fifty-five women's associations were merged in the Women's Organization of Iran (Persian *Sazman-i Zanan-i Iran*) founded under the patronage of Princess Ashraf, Muhammad Reza Pahlavi's twin sister. This organization achieved considerable progress for women, for example, an increase in the minimum age for marriage, measures making it easier for women to get divorces, the legalization of abortion, and a special provision prohibiting a husband from taking a second wife without his first wife's consent. With the exception of female suffrage, nearly all these rights prescribed by the government were revoked after the 1979 revolution, and the wearing of the veil was again made obligatory. At first, the most that could be achieved in the new Islamic Republic was to obtain a certain freedom of action for women. The eight-year war with Iraq (1980-1988) made it necessary to admit women to the world of work and professional activity. Thus at the beginning of the 1990s the debate over equal rights for women was resumed, and many restrictions have in the meantime been toned down, though not the obligation to wear the veil in public. Various women's periodicals reflect new trends seeking to reinterpret Islam in such a way as to bring it into harmony with the modern democratic world or to approach "scientifically" the problem of the inequality of women and by means of Qur'anic exegesis show that in the holy book of Islam no gender-specific discrimination is implied. These publications promote political engagement on the part of Iranian women, whose votes made a decisive contribution to the election of the reformer Khatami to the presidency. It has to be said that moderate clerics do support greater freedoms for women. In the long run, the 1979 revolution has thus produced a new women's movement that is specifically

Iranian and largely free of foreign influences. One of its outstanding figures is the attorney Shirin ʿEbadi (b. 1947), who
was awarded the Nobel Peace Prize in December 2003 for
her activities on behalf of human rights and the improve-
ment of the position of women in Iran. ʿEbadi also regards
her work as firmly rooted in Islam, since—as she emphasized in her Nobel Prize acceptance speech—Iran's serious
shortcomings with regard to human rights and the situation
of women should not be blamed on Islam, but rather on a
mistaken interpretation of the Qurʾan. In 2006, another
movement considerably more distant from Islam launched
the "One Million Signatures Campaign Demanding an End
to Discriminatory Laws against Women." According to its
organizers, this campaign is neither Islamic nor secularist,
and is concerned solely with ensuring equal treatment for
men and women. The future of the Iranian women's movement remains for the time being uncertain.

Future Prospects

With the success of the Islamic Revolution, Iran's long tradition of monarchy, which seems to have become obsolete
under the Pahlavis, has apparently come to a final end. The
attempt, unique in the Islamic world, to set up an Islamic
Republic under the aegis of Shiʾsm has not yet come to an
end. Much will depend on whether it succeeds in solving
Iran's urgent economic problems and in creating some kind
of partnership with the West. There are several ways to carry

out these multi-leveled tasks, ranging from closer cooperation with the West, especially on the economic level, to completely sealing off the country and seeking to create an
autarkic economy based on Islam.

How and whether it will prove possible to reconcile these
divergent tendencies in an Iranian state cannot at this point
be determined. But whatever Iran's future development, one
thing seems certain: although parts of Iranian society may
be alienated from the current regime, for the majority of
Iranians Islam is still inseparable from Iranian identity.
Therefore a democracy based entirely on the Western model,
in which Islam would have a merely subordinate role, will
probably not be established in Iran in the foreseeable future.

Selected Bibliography

General Reference Works

Bosworth, Clifford E. *The New Islamic Dynasties. A Chronological and Genealogical Manual.* Edinburgh 1996.

The Cambridge History of Iran, vols. IV–VII. Ed. J. A. Boyle. Cambridge 1968-1993.

Encyclopaedia Iranica. Ed. Ehsan Yarshaher. New York 1982–2001 (thus far, thirteen volumes reaching as far as the letter "I" have appeared).

Encyclopaedia of Islam (new edition). Selected articles. 12 vols. (complete). Leiden 1960 –2004.

Works on Iranian History

Abrahamian, Ervand. *Iran Between Two Revolutions.* Princeton 1982.

Alfons, Gabriel. *Die Erforschung Persiens. Die Entwicklung der abendländischen Kenntnis der Geographie Persiens.* Vienna 1952.

Algar, Hamid. *Religion and State in Iran 1785–1906. The Role of the Ulama in the Qajar Period.* Berkeley/Los Angeles 1969.

Amanat, ʿAbbas. *Pivot of the Universe. Nasir al-Din Shah Qajar and the Iranian Monarchy, 1831–1896.* London/New York 1997.

Amir Arjomand, Said. *The Turban and the Crown. The Islamic Revolution in Iran.* New York/Oxford 1988.

Avery, Peter. *Modern Iran.* London 1965.

Bakhash, Shaul. *Iran: Monarchy, Bureaucracy & Reform under the Qajars.* Oxford/London 1978.

Bosworth, Clifford E. *The Ghaznavids. Their Empire in Afghanistan and Eastern Iran 994 –1040.* 2nd ed. Beirut 1973.

Bosworth, Clifford E. *The Later Ghaznavids. Splendour and*

Decay. The Dynasty in Afghanistan and Northern India 1040–1186. Edinburgh 1977.

Buchta, Wilfried. *Who Rules Iran? The Structure of Power in the Islamic Republic.* Washington, D.C. 2000.

Frye, Richard N. *The Golden Age of Persia. The Arabs in the East.* London 1975, 2nd ed. 1977.

Halm, Heinz. *Die Schia.* Darmstadt 1988.

Halm, Heinz. *Der schiitische Islam. Von der Religion zur Revolution.* Munich 1994.

Halm, Heinz. *Der Islam.* Munich 1999, 4th ed. 2002.

Hooglund, Eric, ed. *Twenty Years of Islamic Revolution: Political and Social Transition in Iran since 1979.* Contemporary Issues in the Middle East. Syracuse, NY, 2002.

Iran. Natur – Bevölkerung – Geschichte – Kultur – Staat – Wirtschaft. Ed. Ulrich Gehrke and Harald Mehner. 2nd ed. Tübingen/Basel, 1976.

Keddie, Nikki R. (in collaboration with Yann Richard). *Roots of Revolution. An Interpretive History of Modern Iran.* New Haven/London 1981.

Keddie, Nikki R. *Qajar Iran and the Rise of Reza Khan, 1796–1925.* Costa Mesa 1999.

Lambton, Ann K. *Landlord and Peasant in Persia. A Study of Land Tenure and Land Revenue Administration.* London/New York/Toronto 1953.

Lambton, Ann K. *Continuity and Change in Medieval Persia. Aspects of Administration, Economic and Social History, 11th–14th Century.* London 1988.

Lockhart, L. *Nadir Shah. A Critical Study Based Mainly Upon Contemporary Sources.* London 1938.

Löschner, Harald. *Die dogmatischen Grundlagen des schi'itischen Rechts.* Erlangen/Nürnberg 1971.

Manz, Beatrice F. *The Rise and Rule of Tamerlane.* Cambridge 1989.

Matthee, Rudolph P. *The Politics of Trade in Safavid Iran. Silk for Silver, 1600–1730.* Cambridge 1999.

Migeod, Heinz-Georg. *Die persische Gesellschaft unter Násiru'd-Dîn åh (1848-1896).* Berlin 1990.

The Mongol Empire and Its Legacy. Ed. Reuven Amitai-Preiss and David O. Morgan. Leiden/Boston/Köln 1999.

Morgan, David O. *Medieval Persia 1040 –1797.* London/New York 1988.

Richard, Yann. *Der verborgene Imam. Die Geschichte des Schiismus im Iran.* Berlin 1983.

Röhrborn, Klaus-Michael. *Provinzen und Zentralgewalt Persiens im 16. und 17. Jahrhundert.* Berlin 1966.

Roschanzamir, Mehdi. *Die Zand-Dynastie.* Hamburg 1970.

Rubin, Michael. *Into the Shadows: Radical Vigilantes in Khatami's Iran.* Policy Papers 56. Washington D.C., 2001.

Savory, Roger. *Iran under the Safavids.* Cambridge 1980.

Smith, Peter. *The Babi and Baha'i Religions: From Messianic Shi'ism to a World Religion.* Cambridge 1987.

Spuler, Bertold: *Die Mongolen in Iran. Politik, Verwaltung und Kultur der Ilchanzeit 1220 –1350.* 4th ed. Leiden, 1985.

Spuler, Bertold. *Iran in früh-islamischer Zeit. Politik, Kultur, Verwaltung und öffentliches Leben zwischen der arabischen und der seldschukischen Eroberung 633–1055.* Wiesbaden 1952.

Taheri, Amir. *The Spirit of Allah: Khomeini and the Islamic Revolution.* London 1985.

Maps

Historical Atlas of Iran (*Atlas-i tarikh-i Iran,* English-Persian). Tehran 1971.

Tübinger Atlas des Vorderen Orients. Selected maps. Wiesbaden.

Index of Names

149

Breinigsville, PA USA
26 July 2010
242407BV00001B/10/P